Brendan —
It's been a pleasure to encounter your
continually engaging personality, sense of
humor + intellect. As well as your loyal
friendship. Congrats on graduation. Josh

Julio Cortázar
Carol Dunlop

Autonauts of the Cosmoroute

a timeless voyage from paris to marseille

Translated by Anne McLean

with drawings by Stéphane Hébert

archipelago books

Archipelago Books First Edition

Library of Congress-Cataloging-in-Publication Data
Cortázar, Julio.
[Autonautas de la cosmopista, o, Un viaje atemporal París–Marsella. English]
Autonauts of the cosmoroute, a timeless voyage from Paris to Marseilles /
by Julio Cortázar & Carol Dunlop ; translated by Anne McLean ;
with drawings by Stéphane Hébert.
p. cm.
ISBN 978-0-9793330-0-2
1. France – Description and travel. 2. Cortázar, Julio – Travel – France.
3. Dunlop, Carol – Travel – France. 4. Roads – France – Miscellanea.
I. Dunlop, Carol. II. McLean, Anne. III. Hébert, Stéphane. IV. Title.
DC29.3.D8613 2007
914.404'838–dc22   2007027384

Photos by Julio Cortázar and Carol Dunlop and drawings by Stéphane Hébert
reproduced with permission of Julio Silva, in care of Sophie Moret.

Citations from Osman Lins quoted with permission of Dalkey Archive Press
from *Avalovara* by Osman Lins, translated by Gregory Rabassa, copyright 2002.

Archipelago Books
232 Third St. #A111
Brooklyn, NY 11215
www.archipelagobooks.org
Distributed by Consortium Book Sales and Distribution
www.cbsd.com

Cover art: Stéphane Hébert

This publication was made possible with support from Lannan Foundation,
the National Endowment for the Arts, and the New York State Council
on the Arts, a state agency.

We dedicate this expedition and its chronicle

to all the world's nutcases

and especially to the English gentleman whose

name we do not recall and who in the eighteenth

century walked backwards from

London to Edinburgh singing

Anabaptist hymns.

We would like to express our profound gratitude to all those who encouraged us throughout this undertaking with moral and material help, understanding and complicity, and with special thanks to the following people:

Raquel and Jean Thiercelin, the latter known as the 'Raven of Luberon', who immediately offered logistical and every other kind of support from the very conception of the project, and who generously opened their house to the members of the expedition so they could recover from the hardships and tribulations at the end of their voyage.

Necmi Gurmen and Anne Courcelles who, as soon as they heard of the project, agreed to take on the responsibilities of a re-supply mission, and faced up to the most dangerous circumstances to bring fresh provisions to us at the Ruffrey rest stop, where for several hours they shared our living conditions at one of the autoroute's least hospitable parking lots, with a very special thanks to Anne, who applied part of her scientific knowledge to the preparation of a chicken destined to play a leading role in our gastronomic happenings of the following days and who realized, while we were still planning the re-supply mission long before the departure, that those provisions would be more useful if they arrived on Wednesday June 2nd instead of Tuesday the 1st as we'd intended, since on Mondays you can't buy anything interesting in Paris and furthermore that particular Monday was part of a long weekend, all of which had escaped our attention.

Lemi Gurmen, who deliciously confused four apples with four kilos of apples, and who also, the night before departure, advised us to wait for the rescue expedition at the first of the June 2nd stops, thus saving them from having to travel hundreds of extra kilometres since the access to the autoroute to return to Paris was located between the two rest areas in question.

Doctor Hervé Elmaleh and his wife Madeleine, who sensibly warned us of the danger of scurvy that awaited us.

Luis Tomasello, who was not only able to create almost miraculously spacious places for stowing provisions and supplies in Fafner, but who also took care of our cat Flanelle, saving her from having to endure the rough living conditions of the autoroute, not to mention the logistical help he contributed in loading and stowage.

Catherine Lecuillier, who lent us a highly scientific small apparatus, which guaranteed protection against malaria, yellow fever and other plagues, thus assuring us nights of tranquil sleep without the interruptions and tiring, futile frights caused by the presence of mosquitoes.

Nicole Rouen who, travelling towards Paris to her dentist's office on the third day of our expedition, brought us cherries and an interval of pleasant company.

Karen Gordon who, with infinite patience and understanding, helped us with the final preparations, provided us with candies, which we duly savoured, and agreed to forward our mail.

René Caloz, who visited us unexpectedly on the autoroute and generously offered two bottles of *fendant*, providing us with several days worth of delightful aperitifs.

Jorge Enrique Adoum, Françoise Campo, Jérôme Timal, Julio Silva, Gladis and Saúl Yurkiévich, Aurora Bernárdez, Nicole Piché, François Hébert, Hortense Chabrier, Georges Belmond, Laure, Philippe and Vincent Bataillon, Marie-Claude, Laurent and Anne de Brunhoff, who were in on the secret and gave us precious bits of advice that would be too long to list here, and sent us encouraging smiles from afar at the most difficult moments.

The Countess, for many hours of reading filled with emotion.

Brian Featherstone and Martine Cazin, who arrived unexpectedly and saved us from tedium in a particularly stupid rest stop.

Señor and Señora Afonso, who helped so much with our preparations in Paris.

Señora María Martins, who helped us prepare bags and packages with her usual good humour.

All the strangers at the rest areas who, with a smile or friendly gesture, brightened the backdrop of each day.

How to narrate the trip and describe
the river along which – another river –
the trip exists, in such a way that it emphasizes,
in the text, the most hidden
and lasting face of the event, that where
the event, without beginning and without end,
challenges us, moving and unmoving?

Osman Lins, Avalovara

Preambles

O*F HOW WE WROTE A LETTER, WHICH,*
UNUSUAL THOUGH IT MAY HAVE BEEN,
DESERVED A REPLY, WHICH IT DID NOT
RECEIVE, AND HOW IN LIGHT OF THIS, THE
MEMBERS OF THE EXPEDITION DECIDED TO
IGNORE SUCH UNSPEAKABLE BEHAVIOUR AND
BRING TO A SUCCESSFUL CONCLUSION WHAT
WAS DESCRIBED THEREIN IN THE MOST
GALLANT AND DETAILED MANNER

Paris, 9 May, 1982

Monsieur le Directeur
Public Highways Authority
41 bis, Avenue Bosquet
75007 Paris

Monsieur,
Some time ago, your organization requested authorization to publish some passages
from my story "The Southern Thruway" in one of your magazines. I, of course,
granted said authorization with great pleasure.
I am now writing to request in turn authorization of a quite different sort.
My wife, Carol Dunlop – who is also a writer – and I are studying the possibility
of a slightly madcap and quite surreal "expedition", which would consist of travel-
ling from Paris to Marseille on the autoroute aboard our Volkswagen Combi Van,

equipped with everything necessary, stopping at each of the sixty-five rest areas at the rate of two per day; in other words, taking more than a month to complete the Paris–Marseille journey without ever leaving the freeway.

Apart from the small adventure involved, we intend to write a book in parallel with the trip that will describe in a literary, poetic and humorous way the varied phases, events and experiences such a strange journey will no doubt provide. The book might perhaps be called Paris to Marseille in Small Stages, and obviously the autoroute will be its main protagonist.

Such is our plan, which will be carried out with the support of some friends who will be entrusted with replenishing our supplies every ten days (apart from what we can find at the rest stops). The only problem is that, as far as we know, a vehicle is not allowed to stay on the autoroute for more than two days at a time, and for that reason we are writing to you to request the authorization that, when the time comes, would keep us from encountering difficulties at the various tollbooths.

If you think our idea of writing a book on the subject will not be disagreeable to your Authority, and there is no objection to authorizing us to "live" on the autoroute for a month, moving at the rate of two rest stops per day, I would be grateful to receive your reply as soon as possible, since we would like to depart around the 23rd of this month. It should be understood that under no circumstances do we wish our project to be made known to the media since we would not like to see our expeditionary solitude disturbed. When the time comes, our book will endeavour to tell the story to the public in general.

We thank you in advance for your good will with respect to this project, and I beg you to accept, dear sir, my sincere best wishes, as well as those of my wife.

Julio Cortázar

This letter was sent on May 9th, 1982. On the 23rd, after fruitlessly opening our mailbox one last time, we understood that two weeks had been more than enough time for a commercial organization, no matter how plagued with computers and cantankerous secretaries, to respond to our modest request. Looking one another in the eye, we energetically shook hands and said in unison:

"Co-expeditionary, tomorrow at four o'clock in the afternoon we set course for our destination!"

By which we meant that, leaving from Rue Martel, we'd take Rue Petites-Écuries towards République, from there to Austerlitz (good omen!) and after crossing the distance to the Porte d'Italie we would pull out, with characteristic determination, onto the Autoroute du Sud and make our first bivouac at Corbeil.

All of which happened with a precision that surprised even us, since we're both specialists in taking wrong turns and wouldn't have been too surprised to find ourselves on the Autoroute de l'Est or at Place des Victoires. But once heading in the right direction, who could have stopped us? Nobody. Now we could take out the first sandwich and tell each other that we were on our own, incredibly alone, on the first leg of an adventure the reader cannot even begin to imagine, just like us at that moment.

◇　◇　◇　◇

Corollary extracted from The Book of Marvels *by Marco Polo, which will show the reader that in other times, explorers not only received replies to the letters they sent, but also that they were afforded the sort of treatment that our lamentably pallid and paltry times are no longer able to supply.*

And when the Great Khan had charged the two brothers and the baron of the embassy with the commission he was sending to the Pope, he caused to be given them a golden tablet, engraved with the royal seal and signed in the custom of his State, in virtue of which, instead of a passport, the three bearers were emissaries of the Great Khan, entitled to be everywhere conveyed in safety through dangerous places, by the governors of provinces and cities, on pain of disgrace, throughout the whole empire, having their expenses everywhere defrayed, and should be furnished with whatever was needful for them and their attendants in all places, and for as long as they might have occasion to stay, just as if it were He himself who happened to pass that way.

Pierre, our Alpine guide,
who has recovered from his terrible nausea
and has gone back to writing
his memoirs, comes to ask me
to lend him "that which pushes the words
away." It takes me a while to
realize that he's talking about
an eraser.

Jean Charcot, *Around the South Pole*

WHERE THE PATIENT READER

SHALL BE INTRODUCED

TO THE PROTAGONISTS OF THE EXPEDITION,

AND COME TO KNOW THEIR MORE NOTABLE

CHARACTERISTICS AND FEATURES

1

The authors tend to speak among themselves or refer to each other throughout the account of this journey. Naturally they call each other by their first names but also, even more naturally, they frequently resort to their most private names, which they now confide to the reader since they consider it only fair to confide all that has to do with the expedition and the personal lives that sustain it. So it won't be long before references to la Osita, the Little Bear, and el Lobo, the Wolf, begin to appear, and in the case of the latter there is even a fragment of a *Pocket Guide to Lobos* that la Osita was preparing for her own pleasure but also so that el Lobo could be less silly than was his custom and find out a few things that only Little Bears truly know.

Our vehicle Fafner is frequently called the Dragon. Within these pages we will divulge details of his earthly nature, but here it's as well to say that our trio uses its wilderness names not only for reasons of affection and intimacy, but also because during the course of the expedition they identified increasingly with the woods, fields and animals of the freeway's most secret world. It was our fairy-tale side, our innocent ecology, our happiness in full technological clamour, which lovingly obliterated us.

2

*This brief but necessary chapter
is an auto-citation (particularly appropriate word
given the theme) extracted from
a text written years ago and entitled
"Correcting Proofs in Haute Provence".*

And so, every once in a while I stop working and roam the streets, go into a bar, watch what's happening in the city, talk to the old man who sells me sausages for lunch because the dragon – it's about time I introduce him – is a kind of mobile home or snail shell on wheels that my obstinate Wagnerian predilections have designated the dragon, a red Volkswagen van containing a water tank, a seat that folds out into a bed, and to which I've added a radio, typewriter, books, red wine, tins of soup and paper cups, a bathing suit should the opportunity arise, a butane lamp and a camping stove thanks to which a can of something turns into lunch or dinner while we listen to Vivaldi or write these pages.

The dragon thing comes from a long-standing need: I've almost never accepted the names or labels things arrive with and I think that's reflected in my books, I don't see why we should invariably tolerate what comes before and from outside, and so I've given creatures I loved or love names that stem from an encounter, a contact between secret codes, and women became flowers, birds, little animals of the forest, and there are even friends whose names changed after a cycle was complete, the bear could turn into a monkey, like someone with blue eyes was a cloud and then a gazelle and one night turned into a mandrake, but to return to the dragon I'll just say that two years ago as I saw him arriving for the first time, coming up the Rue Cambronne in Paris, fresh from the factory, with his wide red face, low-set sparkling eyes, and a likeable, unruly air, something in me went click and he became the dragon, and not just any old dragon but Fafner, guardian of the treasure of the Niebelungen, who according to legend and Wagner had been evil and stupid, but always aroused a sneaking sympathy in me, if only for being doomed to die at the hand of Siegfried, as I can never forgive heroes for doing that kind of thing, just as thirty years ago I couldn't forgive Theseus for having killed the Minotaur. I have only just now made the connection between these two things; that afternoon I was too busy worrying about the problems the dragon was going to give me in terms of gearshift, height and width far greater than that of my former Renault, but it seems obvious I followed the same instinct to defend those the established order regards as monsters and exterminates as soon as it can. In two or three hours I made friends with the dragon. I told him that as far as I was concerned his name was no longer Volkswagen, and poetry was right on time as usual because when I went to the garage to have his number plate fastened on as well as the initial of the country where I live, all I needed was to see the mechanic screwing a large F on his backside to have my hunch confirmed; of course you can't tell a French mechanic that this letter didn't stand for France but for Fafner, but the dragon knew it and on our way home he demonstrated his delight by jumping up on the sidewalk to the particular fright of a housewife laden with groceries.

3

Where it shall be seen that The Last but Not Least *did not
participate personally in the expedition, but his
priceless contribution confirms, if it were still
necessary, that our trip, rich in wonders,
was also outside of both time and space.*

As soon as our steadfast epic was over – which still hasn't started for the reader whose patience we humbly implore – Fafner had a well-earned rest while la Osita and I left for Nicaragua where we would meet up with Carol's son, who lives in Montréal with his father. Fourteen years old, brimming with joy and his vocation for rock drumming, Stéphane Hébert's adolescent grace added to our happiness during a tropical vacation with our expedition still lingering in our memory like a slightly nostalgic echo.

Stéphane thus discovered our drafts and negatives and contact sheets of the photos from the trip. Carol, familiar with his great talent for drawing, proposed that he become our *ex post facto* cartographer. Stéphane might not have understood the Latin phrase but he immediately took out his pencils and his sketch pad, and got down to imagining each and every one of the rest stops from our texts, explanations, anecdotes and photographs.

The explorers, whose stringency in the matter the reader can easily imagine, marveled at the scientific rigor this teenager brought to his work, and decided to incorporate his relief maps into the general documentation of the voyage. And so, although absent at the time, Stéphane Hébert is as much a presence here as Fafner or ourselves.

CONCERNING THE ORIGINS OF THE EXPEDITION:
ITS GENESIS, ITS SLOW ELABORATION AND SINUOUS FRUITION,
AND WHERE THE READER WILL NOT ONLY SEE HOW SCIENTIFIC
REFLECTION TENDS TO TRANSFORM THE WORLD VISION OF
WHOSOEVER PRACTICES IT, BUT SHALL ALSO NOTICE THE
OBSTACLES THAT RISE UP IN THE PATH OF THE INVESTIGATOR,
AND SHALL AT THE SAME TIME HAVE AMPLE OPPORTUNITY
TO ADMIRE THE SHREWDNESS AND COURAGE OF THE
DARING EXPLORERS

1

Where it shall be seen that the explorers spent several years
on the wrong path, even if it was the same one.

Until the summer of 1978, oh pale and intrepid reader, we belonged to the
race of mortals who take the freeway for what it seems to be: a meticulously
designed modern construction that allows travellers enclosed in their four-
wheeled capsules to cover a distance easily verifiable on a map and generally
foreseen, in a minimum of time and with a maximum of safety. The engineers who conceived and elaborated what could be called the institution
of the freeway performed heroic feats to remove from the driver's path not
only any obstacle that could reduce his speed (it is well known that the vast
majority of users of this route are fanatics for maximum average speed), but
also anything that could distract the driver's concentration from the strip
of asphalt that must give to those who follow it – falsely as we shall prove

in what follows – the impression of uninterrupted continuity, a continuity which eventually includes, after thirty, forty or sixty minutes of constant speed, not only the wheels of the vehicle that the human at the steering wheel still has the illusion of controlling, but also the steering wheel of said vehicle and the hands and reflexes of the human being who thus integrates, consciously or not, that great impersonal totality so sought after by all religions.

It is as well to point out that we both belong to an intermediate species of freewayistas, that is, not only do we make much longer stops than those of the other species, who pause only when the needle of the gas gauge hovers perilously close to the E (or the V, depending on the car) or when their mother-in-law, bathed in tears, says that at her age peeing her pants really would be sufficient reason to change her will; or those who, when the baby goes from green to total white and doesn't even have the strength left to kick the back of the driver's seat as he has been doing for the last three hours to emphasize how hungry he is, stop as close as possible to the freeway to take the sandwiches out of the trunk and eat them as fast as possible and standing up, two metres from a picnic table and sometimes ten metres from a forest full of shade and surprises. No, at least we were among those who take their time, even on the freeway, the ones who look for a nice little corner where we can eat and who yield to the desire to take a siesta, time permitting. We both also like to get off the freeway more than once between the point of departure and that of arrival, which proves that a certain resistance already existed within us to the freeway's insolent pretension that it was the only thing in existence between point A and point B. In my case, I would usually leave it precisely due to this vertigo wherein lies its charm, to break the flight forward at moments when the hypnosis threatens to become total, fatal; in el Lobo's case it's mostly because deep down he doesn't like the freeway, and so he frequently gives in to a nostalgia for green things, for people, for the great calm and slow pace that so often wait on the other side of the tollbooth. For all that, we both appreciate the freeway, even as we reproach it a little for being this necessary evil that we as much as anyone cannot escape in this century of obligatory speed, but we keep our distance, and feel a little sorry for those who become its victims.

To tell the whole truth, oh pale and patient reader, until the summer of 1978, the autoroute didn't seem to have a particular importance for us, and we would even forget all about it for months at a time. It didn't seem called upon to play such an important part in our lives as the Paris Metro, for example, not even as much as certain airlines. Even the *bateaux mouches*, although we never took them, seemed to constitute a more decisive element in our daily life than the freeway. Which is where we were mistaken, and if not for the scientific spirit that predominated during the elaboration of this project, that same spirit that began to provoke its birth, it's possible that our minds would have remained closed forever to this great path that unfurled in vain before our eyes for so many years, in front of our eyes still sealed by ignorance.

2

Where the reader shall see that demons take their holidays in the month of July, and the resulting consequences.

And so the summer of 1978 arrived. In that year – some will still remember – the summer only brightened a few villages in the Midi, while the rest of France was plunged into a dark reign of almost constant rain, and shivered under successive cold spells. Without having consulted the weather forecast (for science too is almost always a case of intuition), el Lobo and la Osita took refuge precisely in one of the few zones where it didn't rain all summer, looking for their share of tranquility and peace, two things of which they'd been cruelly deprived for a long time. (You know, pale and gentle reader, that they did not succumb to the pallor this might have provoked in weaker mortals, that every man and woman who wants to really live their life, rather than be content to watch it as it goes by, runs the risk of losing it at any moment, for reasons that don't necessarily belong to the family of corporeal dangers, and that the bold protagonists of this book had then only just begun to emerge from a time of terrible maelstroms where they'd been on the point of leaving their respective humanities; so do not look upon this withdrawal as simple egotistical laziness, not that there wasn't room for a bit of that as well.)

It was a month, dear reader, in which life and the temperature partook of the same stability: sun, calm, cloudless horizon. There was music, there were fiestas and siestas, and our two characters even managed to sit down at their respective typewriters once again after long months of abstinence. The demons were on vacation and, innocent as only wolves and little bears can be, ours arrived at the conclusion that they had vanquished those forces of evil.

Ah, gentle reader, one must never cry victory, at least not out loud (because demons, a secret we have the duty to reveal in exchange for your great patience, are extremely vain and not very intelligent; if you don't say that you've defeated them out loud, they'll be content with what they consider an efficient policy of harassment, just when their tactics have lost all importance in your eyes. But if you proclaim that they've ceased to impress you, be careful: those beings, who endeavour above all to keep up appearances, will be offended, and the rage that rules them will frequently incite them to call to their aid a whole cohort of more powerful demons, which they can summon should the need arise, despite their laughably tiny size). Later, once we'd learned it well, that rule would spare us many mishaps along the course of the expedition; nevertheless, as the intelligent reader will have guessed by now, in 1978 we hadn't advanced very far on the paths of knowledge, paved with demons as they were.

So much so that from one day to the next, while outside the weather remained unchangingly beautiful, a storm slowly began to build up inside the house. Objects that had been friendly until then started bit by bit to oppose our most insignificant daily gestures: the fridge, which had previously kept us company with the satisfied purring of an ice cube manufacturer, began to roar every time we wanted to listen to a record; hot water began to come out of the tap that had always given us cold water, and vice-versa, producing cries and various traumas; the steps of the stairway began evasive manoeuvres whenever we set foot on them, leaving anyone who thought to climb them lower than where he or she had started the ascent; even the mail changed its nature, and where heretofore we'd read the jubilant tales of friends' vacations and adventures, we found only bad news, threatening bills and balance sheets (every reader who lacks as do we a so-called business sense will understand this last detail); when we asked of the knives only that they cut a peach or the cheese, they arranged to bite us and, while we did acrobatics to avoid their teeth, their friends the forks came from below to jab us.

"Enough!" said el Lobo one day. "Anything, just so long as they leave us in peace!"

"Do you think," asked la Osita, catching in the nick of time a painting that had slipped off the wall and was about to split el Lobo's skull, "we could really live in peace with these infernal and constant aggressions?"

"You'll see," said el Lobo a few hours later, rubbing his cheek where the sheet, which had always perfectly fit the bed in the Midi just as well as the one in Paris, had just leapt up and slapped him in the face as soon as he'd tucked it under the corner of the mattress. "¡*No pasarán!* They shall not pass!"

Everything leads us to believe that the demons (who, let's not forget, came back from their month-long vacation full of energy) viewed that as the worst outrage. They who slip through anywhere were not going to pass? We'd see about that.

More days followed of fierce battles against objects that, if they didn't find an occasion to participate in a direct aggression, would move away ignobly at the moment they were most needed: the papers we'd left on the desk flew off, missing manuscripts would suddenly appear in the oven, not to mention a certain lack of coordination on the part of the demons, for while the fridge had begun to manufacture soup when we needed ice cubes, the oven chilled the raviolis instead of grilling the cheese on top of them.

And one day, going to check something in the boiler cupboard, we let out a shriek: a large bird came flying out. Was this the final sign, the emissary of the dark forces giving us a warning, or rather the last representative of light that, foreseeing the catastrophe, took flight while there was still time? Had it been waiting, since that fatal "*no pasarán*," for someone to open the door? We'll never know, and little does it matter.

Two days later, the dark forces seized Osita, and for days and nights it seemed they'd won the match. However, the demons didn't know that Little Bears soak up light even in the darkness, and as a last resort can even duplicate its intensity, especially when el Lobo, in the shadow of an impassable border, draws them away from the bright side.

When la Osita at last emerged from the gloom, she knew el Lobo had been right to say "*no pasarán*", but she'd also realized how fragile the thin film was in which they'd wrapped themselves to prevent their passing. The experience left our two protagonists physically exhausted, especially after all those ambulances, fears and sleepless nights for them both. Still shaky, they went to stay with their friends the Thiercelins in Serre; demons are not allowed access to Serre, and with the help of serenity and friendship, our future explorers were able to heal their wounds and one day decided to return to Paris, in no hurry since el Lobo saw that la Osita's coat was still a bit sparse and not very shiny. So, fragile as ghosts who aren't sure what they're going to find missing beneath their feet, pure illusion, when they step on the ground, just as illusory, our two protagonists, worn out but fully aware of the true "*no pasarán*", began a return that would give birth to the brilliant idea already known, in other words to the true Paris–Marseille project.

3

Where the reader shall follow our heroes down a path that will involve days full of sunshine, proof of human goodness, and also latent threats; where it shall be seen once again, to quote an illustrious tap dancer, that every cloud has a silver lining, and where our valiant explorers will discover that sometimes it's an advantage not to be anywhere.

Leaving Serre was sad for us. To separate – only because it was necessary – from the magic of the tower, from the tenderness and friendship of Raquel and Jean Thiercelin, from the jokes of their son Gilles, not to mention the encouraging big licks Carlota, their crocodile-dog, lavished upon us in our downcast moments; to separate from the light of the Midi, the long hours of conversation and solitude (the Thiercelins' house is a great mystery where anyone who wishes can become lost, whenever they wish it), was not easy, especially considering the demons – who could never find a fissure in the great walls of Serre, where they never enter – were waiting for us in Paris; they'd even been sending us messages for days to get us to get there as soon as possible (they were bored, poor things, at not being able to resume their outrages and dirty tricks in light of our prolonged absence). So we left against our will, not to please the demons and even less to obey their orders, but rather because obligations of all kinds were awaiting us there that we could not honestly continue postponing.

Embraces, pats on the back, slightly anxious glances, and that gratitude one never manages to express. Fafner full to bursting, one last pat for Carlota, our favourite crocodile, and we watch her go, eyes filled with tears we know to be true, and hide in a corner to sulk.

The solitude found again as soon as we enclosed ourselves in our red capsule was sweet and worrying at the same time. You know, gentle reader, that each time one truly avoids dying, the result is a true birth, even more precarious and painful when one emerges from the darkness with no other mother than oneself, with no other contraction than a will not always fully understood. For a long time the mind remembers the days when it couldn't manage to reach the body or the exterior, and the whole life, without that other view, seems much more fragile than the body that contains it. One surprises oneself advancing by trial and error in a world nevertheless filled with light, returning little by little again to people, as if they might break at the slightest contact, while one feels that the broken fragments within oneself haven't entirely found their places again.

Both of us fragile – for if those trips to the land of gloom tire the travel-ler, they exhaust even more the one who tries to accompany her and crashes again and again against insuperable barriers; not to mention that he has neither the right nor the means to interrupt a permanent existence on the side of light, and the only abandon he is allowed, provided he can allow it to himself, is hope – that's how we left at last, at once sad and happy.

How great ideas are born

It was necessary – first scientific calculations – to make the trip in small stages. We would have liked to take the back roads, but our obligations in Paris wouldn't allow us to take so much time, and we had to respect a certain limit. We decided to take the autoroute, but to leave it every two hours or so to find a good hotel, rest, etc.

(As you'll see, gentle reader, the freeway was still the enemy of repose and of the "pleasant trip" for our poorly illuminated minds; but it didn't take long to change our attitudes.)

We'd only just taken it on when el Lobo decided to stop so we could rest, have a drink and take advantage of the nice weather. So good did we feel ("Isn't it true, Osita, that since we're taking the freeway we have more than enough time?"), that the stop lengthened; we began to glimpse the possibil-ities of the rest areas, at least that one, and at supper time (for the place had shown itself able to adapt perfectly well to the siesta we took inside Fafner, with all the curtains closed), we savoured the delicious things Raquel had slipped into our luggage at the last moment. At nightfall we decided that since we had five days to get to Paris, after all, why not sleep right there. And so we woke up the next morning after an excellent sleep, without hav-ing passed Avignon or maybe even Cavaillon, I can't remember exactly, but I am sure that three days later we still hadn't reached Orange where, at the Orange-le-Grès rest stop, while we carefully observed the ceremony of the men dressed in yellowy-orange overalls and their complicated technique for emptying the garbage cans for the first time, the idea of what would become our Paris–Marseille journey began to germinate.

"How nice it is here," said el Lobo sipping his whisky.

"If only we could keep going at this pace, like stagecoach travellers."

"Stopping for a long time at each rest area . . ."

"We could spend a day in each parking lot, outside the world, imagine, we could relax along this very monster of speed with all the freedom . . ."

"And with no telephone!" exclaimed el Lobo who, as is well-known, suffers from acute telephonophobia.

No one could find us. (Since it was pointless to go and hide on the most remote desert island, because there was always someone who discovers us and who *knows*, from having seen us, where we are. But on the freeway, even if someone recognizes us by chance – and soon you'll see there's no shortage of these coincidences – it would never occur to them that we were *on* the freeway. Quite the contrary, it could serve our cause and send all the demons off on a false trail: "I saw them near Mâcon, they must have been heading for Lyon or Avignon . . ." Who would suspect we weren't going anywhere?)

"Yes," said el Lobo, "but we'd have to do things very scientifically."

"A travel log. Like the early explorers."

"Can you imagine? Describing every rest stop, all the adventures, the people who pass by."

"Another freeway, really."

"Shall we do it, Osita?"

"We shall."

At which point, with a jubilation that might seem exaggerated to the unwarned reader, we began to make up the rules of the game, to choose the most favourable season, even to calculate what we would need to take. At first, and in full innocence of ordinary freewayistas (we weren't even owners of a Michelin map of the autoroutes) we established the following rules: One rest stop per day, no exiting the freeway between Paris and Marseille, and writing a book which on the one hand would incorporate all the scientific elements, the topographical, climatic and phenomenological descriptions, without which said book would lack seriousness; and on the other hand would be in a certain way a parallel book, which we would write following the rules of a game of chance, the methods of which were yet to be established. As for Fafner, he only needed a small refrigerator, in every other way he seemed to us more than adequate.

The rest of the journey we spent observing the freeway with our eyes finally open. It was not just this ribbon of asphalt laid out for speed, punctuated by utilitarian and hygienic stops. No, now we knew it hid something else, and we were determined to discover it. So great was our enthusiasm that on the fifth day we still hadn't managed to reach Lyon, and we had to cover the remaining distance – almost three quarters of the trip – in a single day; but little did it matter to us, since we were returning with a secret treasure. And while el Lobo took care of the steering wheel, la Osita carefully counted the rest stops.

"*How many?*" asked el Lobo incredulously.

"Seventy, give or take a few."

First surprise, oh reader, and first lesson: it was proof that we'd never truly looked at the freeway, since up till then we'd thought there were about thirty parking spots between Paris and Marseille.

The reader will have discerned by now that we're crazy, as well as many other things, but at the same time we have a sufficient sense of reality to realize that never – and now that the experience is coming to an end we regret it – would we have seventy days free to carry out such an expedition. And so, after long deliberation, we decided to modify the rules of the game and make the crossing at a rate of two rest stops per day. In other words (we didn't yet know whether or not other rules would end up imposing a more precise plan) we would have to visit two rest areas each day, passing in each of them a period of time yet to be determined according to the rules as yet undefined (finally, each stop would have to determine for itself the duration of the stop, as will be seen), but always two rest areas a day with the obvious obligation to sleep in the second one, whichever it was. We told ourselves that the essential thing was to spend at least a few hours in each one of those seventy rest areas in order to extract a solid knowledge of each one of them.

Don't think, oh sceptical reader, that we arrived at this decision cheerfully: we already knew the existence of rest areas like the one at Pierre-Bénite and some other mere tongues of concrete right beside the freeway, and at that stage of the plan it would have been easy for us to invent other rules with the object of eliminating them from our route. But just as the zoologist who penetrates the insect kingdom cannot consider himself a true scientist if he rejects from his studies all those insects he finds repugnant, in the same way we must embark on the autoroute with our explorers' eyes as eager to survey its evils as its charms.

The plan becomes concrete

So, in the autumn of 1978, the fundamental bases of the expedition had been set down, with the following rules of the game:

1. Complete the journey from Paris to Marseille without once leaving the autoroute.

2. Explore each one of the rest areas, at the rate of two per day, spending the night in the second one without exception.

3. Carry out scientific topographical studies of each rest area, taking note of all pertinent observations.

4. Taking our inspiration from the travel tales of the great explorers of the past, write the book of the expedition (methods to be determined).

By common agreement, and given that neither of us is a masochist, we decided moreover that we will be allowed to take advantage of all that we can find on the freeway: restaurants, shops, hotels, etc.

Furthermore, and after having carefully studied the issue (we are now in possession of a map of the autoroute that indicates the rest areas, thanks to which we know there are sixty-five of them on the southbound side of the Paris–Marseille route), it seemed impossible to load Fafner with all the provisions necessary for thirty-five days, without risk of succumbing to scurvy or something worse in the course of the trip. We then decided to request logistical support from two pairs of friends, one in Paris and the other in the Midi, who could come to replenish us with fresh supplies on the eleventh and twenty-first day of the journey. It was necessary to choose our accomplices carefully; for a start, such a trip demanded a sacrifice on their part, and only those who had completely understood the meaning and importance of the endeavour would be wholeheartedly willing to help us. Secondly, we had to choose friends as crazy as ourselves, as far as possible, otherwise things could go badly wrong. Thirdly, they would have to have both a car and the necessary time available in order to collaborate. And in the last resort, they obviously had to be true friends, since we were risking our health and even our lives.

On the Midi side there was no hesitation, and we wasted little time in informing the Thiercelins about our project. Not only were they enchanted with the idea, but our valiant Captain Jean offered to come as far as Corbeil to replenish our supplies, if we judged it necessary, offering to travel every three days or even more often if there was anything we lacked. But he soon understood that such frequent visits would somehow affect the seriousness of the expedition – solitary by nature – and it was decided that he would come to our aid only on the twenty-first day once we were already well into the Midi.

A long time went by before we would contact Parisian friends to request the same service. And not because we were short of them but because we had to travel unexpectedly in other directions for different reasons. We told ourselves then that perhaps in the fall, but that autumn we had other obligations, and we swore that in the spring . . . And then the next autumn was upon us, and we intended to leave as soon we got back to Paris but then it turned out Fafner wasn't available for reasons beyond our control, and once again we said we'd go in the spring. Meanwhile, dear reader, don't think we lost heart or sight of the expedition. Quite the contrary, the more our plans were frustrated, the greater our resolve. We kept buying travel books, scientific instruments, we had all the particulars ready; and in the meantime we traveled up and down the autoroute from time to time, a freeway that was now different since we saw it as a territory to be explored, and on each occasion we noticed details that had escaped us until then. In short, and increasingly, we screwed up our courage. How long did it take Columbus to set sail? And Magellan? But let the reader think of the final results of their voyages: a new continent instead of the Indies, and an immense globe instead of a *tabula rasa*. It was worth the wait for the fruits of such determination and patience. We waited four years.

4

Where in spite of the demons we finally arrive at the end
of the prologue, although not without the odd snag.

We still had to find our Parisian accomplices who would help, by providing the logistical support already explained, to ensure our survival. We thought of some and then others while preparations advanced in the little house in Tholonet where we spent the summer of 1981. What do you think of . . . ? Yes, but they're on vacation right now and I don't know if we could explain things by letter . . . And . . . ? Mmm, I think they're going away in the fall. And . . .? Oh, they'd send us straight to a psychiatrist . . .

That's what we were up to one day when we heard in the distance, on the dirt road that led to the cottage, a *ptuf-tuf* that could only belong to a Volkswagen beetle, and not one of the younger ones. We went out onto the balcony and, oh miracle of miracles, who did we see emerging from a cloud of dust? Fafnerito, natural son of Fafner by decision of his owners, an archaic survivor of a time when cars were made to last, as you could see from all the scars on his shell; Fafnerito who, thanks to a particularly heroic feat, brought us Anne Courcelles and Necmi Gurman, who got out of the car dying of laughter and swatting themselves energetically to get rid of the dust.

Lobo's eyes met Osita's, and all was concluded in the space of that glance.

Without any doubt, Necmi, our favourite Turk, and Anne, his sweet and lively companion, filled all the conditions.

1. As far as being friends, they were (and are, as will be seen) true ones.

2. As for madness, see their arrival in Tholonet in a car that should never have gone further than Port d'Orléans.

3. They had a car, so to speak.

4. Both possessed an ever-present sense of humour, which would surely incite them to participate with great enthusiasm.

5. In view of free time, it might be a little tricky, since Anne bravely traveled by train every morning to try to inject a little intelligence into brains that absorb brandy with more ease than they do Latin or Greek, but knowing her goodness and joyful personality, we trusted she'd be able to invent a little cold if necessary so that Necmi wouldn't hog all the glory of such an illustrious supply mission.

Consequently, and after offering them a stiff drink to facilitate things, we made our proposal. (I regret that current technology does not allow the inclusion of cassettes in normal editions of books, for words can never express the laughter that immediately invaded Necmi's entire body and must have been heard on the other side of Mount Sainte-Victoire.)

We had triumphed.

Or almost.

Because, as we've told you before, gentle reader, one must never cry victory, and especially in the month of August, as has been seen. Four years after seizing la Osita, the dark forces pounced, savage and implacable, on el Lobo, who emerged, many days later, from the gloom. And so once more, instead of Paris–Marseille from rest area to rest area, we had to return to the light step by step, and once more the Thiercelins opened their house (not for nothing did it previously belong to the Hospitaliers), where life, like last time, slowly, prudently recommenced.

And it took shape, to such an extent that even before leaving Serre, where we were joined by Luis Tomasello who'd come to look after us as if we weren't just his friends but his children, we decided that the Paris–Marseille project, which over the years had attained the dimensions of an essential, mystical project, *would be carried out in the spring*. Even before buying an appointments diary for 1982, we knew that a good six weeks between May 20th and the end of June would be blank. No journey, no matter where, no work, *nothing* would keep us from doing it. Somehow, to prove we could carry out this trip was to prove to ourselves that we had weapons against the gloom, not just in its large manifestations like the one that had just left us so fragile, but also in its more insidious expressions, the banality of daily obligations, those commitments that mean nothing in themselves but all together distance us from that center where we all hope to live our lives. We took Julio's illness as a warning. Not to live life in its truest way is a crime, not just against oneself, but against others as well.

For that reason, with Luis's help, we took advantage of the weeks of convalescence and the calm of Serre (where, as has been mentioned, demons don't cross the threshold, though ghosts wander around at will) to get Fafner in good shape, secure the fridge properly, and build a storage cupboard for the provisions that would ensure our survival between supply missions.

From then on, pale and intrepid reader, we remained firm. No invitation was accepted, despite the campaigns waged with a view to obtain el Lobo's presence in some place or another in the months of May and June (and it wasn't easy, since it was impossible to give an acceptable explanation for our refusal). They did not pass. We did. With hope, oh patient companion of these pages, that our experience has opened some doors for you too, and that some parallel freeway project of your own invention is already germinating.

Imagine a river voyage.
The boatman, from source to estuary,
follows the flow of the waters. Does that
passage begin? Does it end? The boatman
thinks that's how it is and that's how it looks: and in
truth there's an aspect of the passage where
the beginning and the end do exist,
where a reading or execution
of the voyage exists. There is an aspect of the voyage where
past and future are real; and another,
no less real and more difficult to find, where
the voyage, the boatman, the river,
and the extension of the river mingle.
The oars of the boat cut
the whole length of the river at one time;
and the voyager, forever and since
always, begins, undertakes, and concludes
the voyage in such a way that the departure
at the headwaters of the river does not
come before the arrival at the estuary.

Osman Lins, *Avalovara*

HOW THE EXPLORERS EQUIPPED FAFNER
WITH THE SUPPLIES ESSENTIAL FOR
AN UNDERTAKING ON SUCH A SCALE,
AND THE DETAILED ENUMERATION THEREOF
GENEROUSLY TRANSMITTED TO OTHER AUTONAUTS
WHO MIGHT ATTEMPT SIMILAR CROSSINGS

Determined to make the expedition as scientific as possible, el Lobo takes it upon himself to consult eminent travel books in order to equip Fafner with adequate provisions. The diary of Captain Cook – whose surname was already quite promising – supplied the following information worth noting:

> *I have already indicated the constant preoccupation of the Navy and Victualling Boards to furnish us with the very best of stores and provisions that experience or authoritative advice leads us to consider as favourable for the health of the sailors; I shall not abuse the patience of my reader repeating the entire list, and limit myself to the most useful.*
>
> *We were provided with a supply of malt, with which we prepared the* mosto dulce; *of this we distributed two pints a day, which was sometimes increased to almost three, as the surgeon sees necessary, who orders us to add a supplement to such persons as have got the scurvy, or whose habit of body threatens them with it. It is indubitably one of the best antiscorbutic medicines so far discovered, and I am persuaded that applied in time it can prevent the disease from worsening, although I do not believe it could actually cure it on the high seas.*

Sauerkraut, of which we had a great supply, is not just a wholesome vegetable but also a great antiscorbutic food, and close packed in casks will keep a good long time; on the high seas each sailor was served a pound twice a week, but I increased or diminished their allowance as I thought proper.

Portable tablets of broth . . .

"Hang on a second," said Carol. "If we're going to have to spend more than a month swallowing disgusting things like that, I'd rather stay home."

"But Captain Cook says . . ."

"Before you finish your useless sentence, I suggest you come with me to the grocery store on the corner, which might not be the Navy and Victualling Boards but on the other hand is full of things as delicious as they are antiscorbutic."

And so it was that two days before our departure we entered this establishment already well known to us, and which had the notable advantage of being located a few doors away from the garage in whose basement waited, pawing the ground, our red dragon Fafner. Before the stupefaction of the cashiers we filled two wagons to the brim and went down the street with them to the admiration of plenty of neighbours and passersby. This process was repeated half an hour later, when the checkout girls had alerted the manager who, just in case, carefully monitored the payment of the provisions, an inventory of which follows in no particular order, since each of us had a different list based on our respective predilections and gastronomical specialties.

This is what we took:

Whisky by the litre	Salt, pepper
Wine, ditto	Rye bread
1 dozen eggs	Jam
2 bottles mineral water	Breakfast biscuits
Grated parmesan cheese	Rice
Butter	Spaghetti

Oil
Vinegar
Nescafé
Desserts (canned fruit, custards)
Ham
Tuna
Sardines
Mayonnaise in a tube
Corned beef
Tinned corn, peas, chickpeas,
    beans, mixed vegetables
Tinned sauerkraut

Tomato sauce
Various cheeses
Tinned couscous
Fresh fruit
Onions
Lettuce
Tomatoes
Cleaning products
Paper to dry dishes
Toilet paper
Sponges

The fresh products were purchased in small quantities, for they would not last long. Our friends who would have to re-supply us on the tenth and twenty-first days had instructions to provide us almost exclusively with:

Fruit
Butter
Cheeses
Vegetables
Meat
Bread (baguettes)

For the whisky and other aperitifs we had a soda siphon with gas canisters, which saved us from multiplying the number of bottles.

We also took a very small quantity of chocolate, but we avoided all luxuries in terms of sweets, sure that an expedition of this nature must be undertaken with austerity. We won't say anything about pharmaceutical matters and the first-aid kit, because in these cases each of us has our own personal ailments, but we didn't forget that on the autoroute there are no drugstores, so we had to anticipate every eventuality.

The Expedition

14:12 Somewhere in the 10th arrondissement of Paris, in
the rain.
Last details, inspection of cargo. Water supply in
jerry can, since hand pump is not working well and the
tank is unfit for use. International assistance at the
departure: Luis Tomasello and Karen Gordon.

14:25 Departure in the rain.

14:44 Take bypass at Porte d'Italie. Rain.

14:47 ENTRY ONTO *L'AUTOROUTE DU SUD*.

15:10 Stop: AIRE DE LISSES.
Wind, sun, clouds. 17°C.
Fafner facing: N.N.W.
Elf Service Station.
Small hills in the distance. Towers on the horizon.
Many, many English tourists.

17:54 Dramatic hailstorm.

 <u>Dinner: rather sumptuous given the circumstances: cold
meat, celery root, beets, corn, bread, coffee.</u>

18:28 Stop: AIRE DE NAINVILLE.
Arrival during furious storm. Impossible to explore the
surroundings given the intensity of the rain.
Wooded rest area. Thunder and lightning.

20:00 Waking up from a well-earned siesta, the weather is
fine. Birdsong. There is a clearing in the rest area. We
observe a hare as large as a small dog, the colour of a
hen, who leaps as if trying to imitate the flight of a
butterfly.

Initial Discouragement

The truth is we're a little overwhelmed by this beginning of the trip in which the scientific obligations confront a considerable *dolce far niente*, tons of books to read, the preparation of reports that, in the future, you will be reading in the present, which for us will already be long past; and what's more, cook, drive the indomitable Fafner, keeping him on a tight rein from rest stop to rest stop (at two per day this is the least important, but the dragon will get offended if we don't point out his role as third author right from the start).

The result of such understandable beginners' discouragement is:

The solemn, though slightly disorganized, moment of departure. Friends and assistants deal with some last minute verifications.

momentary confusions, collisions when we both reach for the packet of cigarettes lost behind bags and stuff at the same time, tendency to circle around the shrubbery, as good translators of English novels put it, punitive incursions into the bottle of Glen Mavis blended and bottled in Scotland, and meals prepared with a certain tendency towards confusion and splashes. But we already know: if we stay this overwhelmed over the whole course of the journey, it will be a total success.

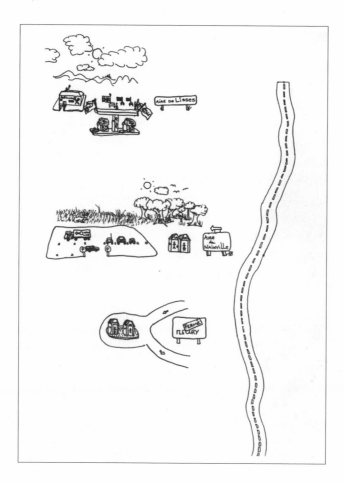

47

Aᴜᴛᴏʙᴀᴘᴛɪsᴍ

This parallel highway we're looking for perhaps only exists in the imagination of those who dream of it; but if it exists (it's too soon to make categorical affirmations, and nevertheless one would say *we're there* and have been for the last twenty-four hours; let the sceptical reader think, before denying reality to this new route by eliminating the "perhaps" from the phrase, that maybe we'll disappear with it; may he have patience then, at least wait until we've been able to gather the evidence), it doesn't just involve a different physical space but also another time. Cosmonauts of the autoroute, like interplanetary travellers who observe from afar the rapid aging of those who remain subject to the laws of terrestrial time, what are we going to discover when we go at camel speed after so many trips in airplanes, subways, trains? (There was, it's true, that long boat trip from San Francisco to Le Havre, but everything happened there, as it should on the ocean, at the speed of the sea, and no one passed us at full throttle as happens here.) *Autonauts of the Cosmoroute*, says Julio. The other path, which is, in any event, the same one.

Faced with inclement weather, the explorers practice various manoeuvres ...

. . . designed to test the team and equipment on board. (Archères-la-Forêt)

7:30 Beautiful morning. 19°C.

  Breakfast: orange juice, madeleines, coffee.

8:59 Sabotage? The FLEURY rest stop is closed.

  Obliged to continue until the next.

9:03 Stop: AIRE DE ARCHÈRES-LA-FORÊT.

  (The forest is beyond the boundaries of the rest area).
  We search with difficulty for a place to settle the dragon;
  the only convenient site (behind the service station)
  flaunts a No Parking sign. We take up the gauntlet. Sun
  shining. The thermometer is not working.
  Fafner: Prow facing south.

  Lunch: fried eggs with cheese, salad, cheese, apples.
  Service station with shop: the "Samaritaine" of the
  highway: you can even buy televisions (and jars of
  mustard in the shape of toilets) there.
  The actual toilets are clean, and there's paper.
  Hot water.
  Contact with civilization: Newspapers!
  In the Malvinas, the English and the Argentines are
  killing each other ever more savagely, according to
  the radio.
  We observe an abnormal quantity of magpies who give the
  impression of wanting to disguise themselves as zebras.
  Their number increases as the lunch hour approaches.
  Magpies in pajamas, says Julio. N.B. This rest area
  counts for two, given the sabotage noted above. Beautiful
  morning, then it clouds over and rains again. Julio buys a
  tube of glue to fix the wing mirrors, the tube is empty. Can
  you glue glass with air in a tube? Change Fafner's oil at
  65,888km. Siesta rather disturbed by monsters that pass

by brushing up against us and growling, but Fafner knows
how to defend us.
The weather improves in the afternoon, but the grey
persists.
Carol has now tried out every WC on the ladies' side, and
confirms that all are equally efficient.
Lovely end to the day, cool, bright.
El Lobo has prepared a sumptuous repast.

    Dinner: *petit salé aux lentilles*, cheese, apples.

The water pump is definitely broken, and as far as we can see there's no way to fix it. We bless (in our way, without crossing ourselves or evoking supreme beings, but smiling as we raise the jerry can to pour water on the sponge glove with which we can improvise an extremely necessary "bath" after twenty-four hours on the road, after our siesta; and the smile achieves what the madeleine we ate this morning could not in the Nainville rest area, where we didn't see a single *nain*: the jerry can tilts and here again is our last departure from the Midi, Jean's embrace beneath the autumn sun, Raquel with her arms full of thyme and marjoram), we wholeheartedly bless Captain Thiercelin, farsighted and generous donor of said jerry can, which only our mistrust of the water pump led us to fill at the last moment, to discover now that water flows almost as well from a jerry can as from a tap.

Now that this important hygiene issue is resolved, how shall we proceed? Apart from the fundamental rules of the game, we haven't got the slightest clue. Write. But maybe not directly: events need a little time to turn into words. As if their sense, and even their form, should travel a long interior path before finding their cohesion.

Will we have to force ourselves to work? Now that we're fully in the thing, we realize that what was conceived as an adventure could too easily be lived as a simple month-long vacation. The sudden freedom from telephone, mail, obligations, etc., counts for a lot, of course. For the moment we feel our way in the surprise of having *actually* left; for the rest it would be boasting to pretend that we're absolutely sure we'll last the thirty-three days. Be that as it may, before opening our typewriters with some nervousness, we've consulted the Tarot, thinking we might discover there some lines of the game, and also thinking that in a certain sense we'd see the great lines of the journey.

With all the cards face down, we turn up three in the following order: Hermes' Chariot; the Fool; the Emperor.

Hermes' Chariot: Victory, but in order to attain it, physical and moral forces must be well-balanced. Knowledge of adversities and the readiness to overcome them. Success, advances on merit. Political dissent, disruptions and revenge have now been defeated. Conquest. The seeker arrives at the summit of success and popularity. Tact for governing. This card also indicates mobility, journeys, progress.

The Fool: Madness, rashness, extravagance. Silliness. Ridiculous acts. Obsession. Frivolity. Total abandon.

The Emperor: Represents for the seeker the support necessary to realize his hopes. Indicates firmness, positivism, an indomitable will. Honesty, vigor; could be a good executive. Authority. Triumph. Sign important contracts. Harmonious situations, emotional as well as professional. Stable health.

WHERE EL LOBO PLAYS WITH FIRE

First signs of fate at the Archères-la-Forêt rest area. On the one hand, the message that comes to us from the Tarot (Carol officiating, both of us a little startled) could not be more encouraging. When I turned over the three cards and saw the Chariot of Hermes, I knew. All that comes from this subtle god has always guided me in life, and if being a Virgo is not exactly comfortable on many levels, on others, the mercurial, the grey, the introverted have often given me something like the itineraries of a mole in bright sunshine, passages through where many Taureans and Capricorns would have broken their horns. Now I know we are going to reach our goal,

A little lost among so much touristic enthusiasm, Fafner raises his roof as high as it will go so we can see him from afar.

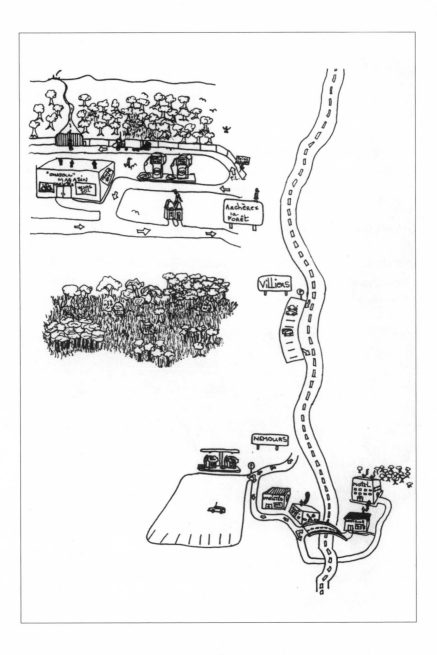

that Hermes will have a little fun at our expense, but at the same time will be making way, lord of the roads, protector of travellers.

On the other hand, a fragrant sign at five-thirty in the afternoon. Considerably depressed by the Spanish edition of a book by Werner Herzog, I went to get some air on the north side of the rest area, where a patch of wasteland full of auspicious little flowers leads to a paved path that rises to a pavilion undoubtedly reserved for the manager of this particularly important rest area with its full-service garage, a shop with somewhat surprising products (would you buy a television on a freeway?) and other facilities I can't always quite figure out.

When I arrived at the top of the path, the perfume of a tree covered in white flowers was like a voice telling me: "You see, this isn't the smell of the autoroute anymore, here's the entrance to another world." However, it wasn't about entering but leaving, and that was at once the sign and the temptation: almost incredibly, in this closed microcosm that joins Paris to Marseille, on this endless succession of eight hundred kilometres of wire fences, embankments, barriers, hostile hedges and other French-fabricated great walls of China, at this initial, almost virginal stop of our voyage, I found myself before a gate chained and padlocked, but at the same time and for reasons I'll never comprehend, offering a passage that had something of the entrance to a labyrinth about it, an incitement to cross, to go around a first bend and then a second that opened onto a dirt path between crops on the other side, and in the distance the vision of a small village less than a kilometre away.

So obvious, almost rude. Once again, Temptation. No tree or snake or apple, but the invitation to go through the passage and violate, without anyone knowing, the rules of the game, for no reason, for the pleasure of advancing ten or twenty metres and returning to our territory. For shit's sake, as the shit-disturbers say. Not to tell Carol, for example, keep this transgression to myself like we keep most of them. Or to tell her, maybe. Yes, it was a sign, but unlike the Tarot, a sign inviting me to exercise my liberty.

On my way back (did I exercise it in one sense or another? You decide), thinking once more like *homo ludens*, I was sort of grateful for not having changed, almost at the end of life, on that plane so many others replace with solemnity or playing the stock market. I remembered games at eight, ten years of age: this is allowed, this is not allowed, without any explanations or reflection, kite season started in such and such a month and no one, in the vacant lots of Banfield, the town of my childhood, would have considered flying theirs before that initial date that no one known had ever fixed either, before or after that period which opened and closed in obedience to an unknown tradition. I remember the rules of hopscotch, tag, marbles, and the gradual admission of other rules that started enclosing me in the world of grown-ups, those of ludo, checkers, chess: You-can't-castle-while-you're-in-check, touch-move, all established, fatal and perfect like two plus two is four or the liberating bells of General San Martín. So today, and on the 32 days we have left, we-cannot-leave-the-autoroute.

Oh yes, it was a good sign, it's done me good finding it enveloped in the perfume of the bush with the white flowers. True gerontology, to feel again "that twenty years is nothing", and many more than twenty, *compadre*.

Seen from childhood (or at least going back there in memory) when play-ing was an obligation, the rules that determined everything seemed to exist since time immemorial, and if you dared to point out that someone had taken it upon themselves to *invent them* . . . watch out, subversive child! Entering into the game, when we're not talking about make-believe – I'll be the King and you be the Indian, for there the "rules" did fluctuate with the rhythm of the imagination, but only very solid friendships survived them – was perhaps the least painful apprenticeship of that loss of liberty we associate (uselessly?) with growing up, "living in society" where the rules are no less arbitrary, at least for the most part (safeguard of everyday life, *who* decided everything has its limits?), than those of hopscotch (couldn't it be played in a circle, including trees, skyscrapers, or enlarging the borders of the drawing when the pebble falls on one side?).

Unbendable rules, and no one knew why. You had to look for really exceptional circumstances (or play by yourself) to be able to change them; playing hopscotch on the slope of a hill, for example, would at least let you add invented rules – if the stone rolled to the right, miss a turn, if it rolled left, you can jump further, and if a little avalanche sweeps it all away, the first one home wins – and change the world.

One way to force you to cheat, perhaps, which was the only exit games had. But real games of transgression, those you play alone. Of course, there were the minor transgressions that everyone expected, the adults first of all, and that you could share with your friends. But profound, intimate, constant transgression, that freedom taken on very early to refuse the world if need be? The best thing was for no one to know anything. Only later did we learn to establish with total freedom our own games with their silent and essential rules. To give reason to things, when necessary. Sketches of some paths that if not for the rules would have been just barren imagination or nothing at all. This trip, without its rules, would be nothing more than stupidity (crossing the country from Paris to Marseille is of interest only for sight-seeing, while making the journey . . .) But do we have to believe that a rule loses its force if it's infringed?

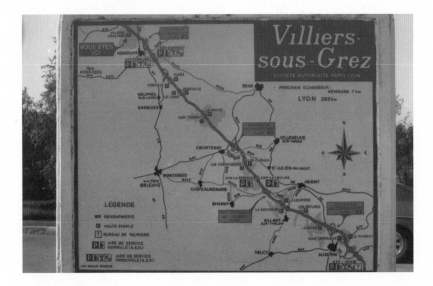

Was it out of perversity that you suggested I take a walk over by the fragrant tree? The little gate was ajar; on the other side a narrow path, three tiny houses, a doghouse and a clothesline with a sheet and two or three shirts hanging from it. Postcard from the year 2050: view of suburbs in the last quarter of the previous century.

Is that why I ran all the way across the field until I got back to the van? It was certainly not because that gate frightened me. And we cut the apple in two at lunchtime.

Breakfast: orange juice, madeleines, coffee.

8:34 Departure with magnificent weather.

8:44 Stop: AIRE DE VILLIERS.

Fafner: Prow facing south.

We park in one of two strips parallel to the autoroute.
Towards the left, vast wooded area where there are many:
tables/benches/megaliths (rocks from the Fontainebleu
region)/carved rocks (probably modern but you never
know)/slopes/rolling hills/pine trees/birds/etc. The
most beautiful rest area so far. In the distance, valleys
and hills. Nearby, a great number of English tourists who
so far vastly outnumber the Belgians, which is surprising.

11:00 Big surprise! Nicole Adoum arrives, on her way to
Switzerland. She brings us cherries and affection.

Lunch: tuna salad with peppers, tomatoes and onion,
cheese, custard, coffee.

Carol goes to distribute the rest of the bread to the
birds and hears our first cuckoo of the trip.

15:40 Departure.

15:50 Stop: AIRE DE NEMOURS.

Fafner facing: E.N.E.

We sleep in the motel.

Dinner: steak-frites, coffee (in the motel).

Last night, in our first motel, longing for a shower and a decent bed, we enjoyed for a few hours the technological, gastronomical and hygienic privileges of a modern facility. The TV at the foot of the bed put scenes from the Malvinas War before our eyes, abolishing distance in the offhand way of electronic machines. Switches, keys, faucets, every implement afforded us its quota of comfort, while mattresses and pillows offered the sweet trilogy of love, rest and sleep. It's always like this, you gradually enter a zone of pleasure and security that dissipates the feeling of precariousness always latent on the street, in the car, out in the open and in crowds. Maybe that's why – we should have kept it in mind – the Devil's attack is more horrible when it happens mid-celebration, when evil chooses good's territory to infiltrate and strike.

It happened after a short while, when we wanted to toast our first motel of the autoroute and looked in the mini-bar of the room for the two ritual bottles of whisky and ice cubes. I filled a glass for Carol, prepared mine, and we sat down to drink and smoke after the hot bath we'd so badly needed. When I tasted my whisky, I knew instantly that I'd fallen for the old, oft-repeated trick. Only then did I realize that my mini-bottle had opened easily, while Carol's had resisted as all properly sealed lids do. My drink was the colour of whisky, but urine can be that colour, too.

I went to the bathroom, rinsed out my mouth, and opened a little bottle of Martini, which I checked carefully and found perfectly sealed. Carol generously tried to minimize that slight but repugnant horror. It couldn't have been urine but shampoo or something, any yellowish liquid that looked like whisky. It didn't matter much anymore, though I was sure, I saw what Argentines call a *ranada*, a cunning trick or a practical joke, and who knows

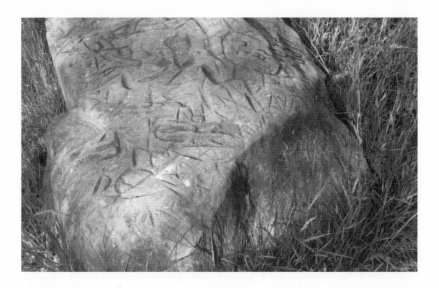

The mysterious carved rocks of the Villiers rest area (see Champollion and other experts).

In the calm of Villiers, the freeway begins to lose consistency.

Other people's autoroute, seen from l'Aire de Villiers.

what Mexicans or Danes or Italians call it but it's always the same, piss in a bottle of beer or whisky, leave it looking intact and enjoy the double pleasure of not paying for the drink and anticipating the expression or nausea of the invisible but certain victim, in the near future inevitably bound, condemned to fall into that clever trap.

I'm not a bad guy – I don't think so, anyhow – but I never deny myself a just revenge, even if it's only mental. I think that it's possible to project a desire and that it will somehow be fulfilled, just as Keats says in one of his letters that it's always good to make prophecies because they find a way of making themselves come true later. I thoroughly desired that the perpetrator of the prank would crash somewhere on the freeway, that his car would end up like Juan José Mosalini's *bandoneon* when he wraps it around his knee on the last chord of a tango, and that the driver would not suffer any serious injuries. No serious injury, no, but later the doctors would diagnose an irreversible hypouremia or, just as good, a piercing macrocystitis, that meant he could only piss drop by drop, drop by drop into one of those tiny sample bottles; the doctors would need to analyze the laborious dose of urine daily and decide that in any case it was not Johnnie Walker Red Label.

Unexpected but very welcome visitor, Nicole Adoum, learns with understandable stupefaction of the explorers' plans.

View from the bridge at l'Aire de Nemours: the freeway flees into the distance, but we stay put.

Aire de Nemours motel. A shower! A bed!

Room 103 of the Nemours Motel.

Letters from a Mother (I)

My dear Eusèbe,

Your father and I are very happy to have your news and to hear that your trip went well. Here, it's the usual routine as you can imagine, but at least we're having a splendid spring. It already feels like summer and often, in the afternoons, when we have our limeflower tea on the balcony, it saddens me to think how much you would have enjoyed this weather. But your father calls me to order, reminding me that in his day people weren't so sensitive, and the option of working abroad didn't even exist, just military service in very tough conditions . . . But you've heard all that from him many times, so I won't repeat it.

We were going to go away for the weekend, maybe to the forest of Fontainebleau, but your cousin André came to visit and, along with your father, started watching the tennis on television, then after lunch papa said we could at least go for a drive, but imagine (you know André, it's a shame but I could never understand how Jacqueline could have married so badly, and there's nothing to be done, there are children who take after their fathers), with all the wine they'd drunk at lunch, I wasn't about to get in the car with your father behind the wheel, so we just stayed home.

Anyway, yesterday we went to see Aunt Héloïse in Ury. She's the same as ever, poor thing, but our visit seemed to please her. Obviously your father insisted on taking the autoroute so we'd get there faster. We had to stop to get gasoline, since he hadn't thought of it earlier; you really shouldn't dare go onto the freeway if you haven't thought of everything. Just imagine: we could have run out of gas in the middle of all those people racing past at hundreds of kilometres per hour without batting an eye. Anyway, while your father was asking the mechanic to check I don't know what, I got out of the car to stretch my legs. I don't understand anything of those conversations with mechanics, and I've never understood why he has to talk about every little thing inside the car every time we stop for gas. Your father spends all the time he saves by taking the freeway talking to those people. Personally, I much prefer the back roads where there are trees, but I'm not the one who does the driving. Walking around the rest area, I saw a strange couple, who perhaps might have interested you, given your profession. They reminded me of your Aunt Rosa and her husband, remember? I don't know if you'd remember them, you must have been six or seven when she died, and her husband didn't survive her for long. Rosa must have weighed a hundred kilos, and she was at least two metres tall. Nobody ever figured out who she took after, you know how in our family we all have rather delicate constitutions. In any case, and contrary to what everyone expected, when she was twenty she decided to go dancing in spite of everything . . . and she came home with a fiancée! It goes without saying that we didn't bother asking him for reference letters, and three weeks later they were married. Oh, but you should have seen them! She, the bride, had decided to be married in white and all the rest, I assure you she was imposing, and he who really looked like that bearded painter, the one who painted scenes from the seedy side of life, to such an extent that I've never seen a single one of his paintings, when he arrived at the town hall in his tail coat we felt like standing him up on a chair so he could look his bride in the eye. But anyway, believe it or not, they were happy till the end, and that's more than you can say about most couples. But what was I talking about? Oh, yes, behind the service station there was one of those house-trucks they make these days. Not a real truck, more like a small van, but completely fitted out to spend the weekends, with a sort of tent that lifts out of the roof. And there, behind the service station, there was a couple all set up as if they'd reached the place they were going to spend their vacation. He was very tall – handsome, I should say, bearded but not like a hippie or any of those people, a perfectly respectable looking fellow with a nice face – and she was so tiny at his side that if you were tempted to think naughty thoughts, you'd wonder how they did certain things . . . I thought at first that they'd come from far away and were resting after having crossed Paris, but I noticed the car had a Paris registration number (I recognize the 75 plates because your father always vents his fury at them when he's behind the wheel, and shouts "filthy Parisians" or something

69

worse). Do you think they were an illegitimate couple? What a place for that kind of adventure! But they seemed nice, they smiled at me and then we left, I tell you Héloïse is not at all well.

Well, my dear boy, I'd better stop here because it's almost five and I haven't started to make dinner yet. Take good care of yourself. We send you all our love,

Maman

(to be continued)

Breakfast: orange juice, croissants, bread, butter, jam, coffee (in the hotel).

9:58 Departure.

10:08 Stop: AIRE DE SONVILLE. Beautiful rest area.

Lunch: corned beef, chickpea salad, cheese, cherries.

14:35 Departure beneath a scorching sun.

14:45 Stop: AIRE DU LIARD.

Lovely wooded rest area. There is a big field, flowers, tall grasses, and at the far end we find a little beach. We don't swim, suspecting crocodiles.

16:00 Surprise! René Caloz arrives, having found out about the trip and stopped in every single rest stop since Paris until he found us. When he goes he gives us two bottles of *fendant*.

Dinner: a Chinese dish, lychees in syrup, coffee.

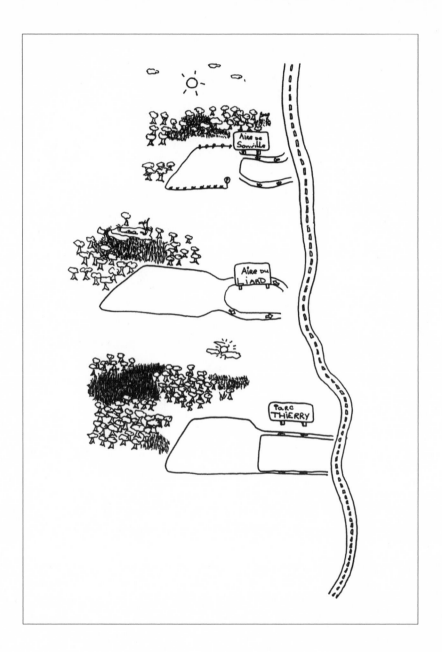

WHERE THE TRAVELLERS WONDER IF
ABSOLUTE SOLITUDE IS POSSIBLE.
EXAMPLES PROVING IT'S NOT:
– EXPECTED AND INEVITABLE VISITORS
– UNEXPECTED VISITORS
– CONVERSATIONS AND GIFTS

It's well known that wherever I might be, including the possibility of a space capsule on its way to Mars, Jacques Cousteau's bathyscaphe or those Tibetan temples where only yaks and abominable snowmen live, Calac and Polanco will appear at some moment with the incessant intention of destroying our resonant silence, the silence that's golden, and the restful life of one who flees from the madding crowd and follows (in this case) the hidden path of the Southern Thruway.

Poor little Osita is entirely innocent of this recurrence of the Tartars, as I've always called them due to their devastating customs when it comes to cohabitation and especially gastronomy, but I cannot evade my personality. Without pausing to weigh up the consequences of my actions, I allowed Calac and Polanco into several of my books where they walked around as if over conquered territory, and now it's even logical that they should brusquely barge into this chronicle and almost immediately inform us that they've decided to follow our route and look out for our safety even at the price of the highest sacrifices.

However, while it's true that I have allowed them into many of my writings, it's no less true that I have always done my utmost to get them to leave, something I haven't always achieved. La Osita puts up with them because

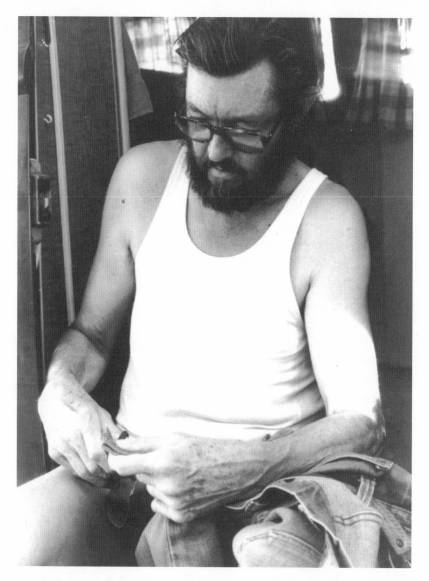

El Lobo decides to take drastic measures to deal with the heat wave: he cuts his blue jeans and turns them into shorts.

Our dragon broaches his first conversations with trees and birds.

they claim to be (and actually are) friends of mine, and now she offers them a drink, which they accept in their usual offhand manner. Since I know them, I don't give them the pleasure of asking how they managed to find us at this rest area, and opt for attributing it to chance, apart from which I pretend not to know of their intentions to watch out for us, as they say. Experience has taught me that the Tartars in some way depend on me, that is if I don't get careless while I write and don't let myself get carried away by any old mental association that brings them back, I can be sure we won't see them again until the end of the expedition. They know it although they pretend the opposite, and they cast sidelong glances at me, at me and at the bottle of scotch Osita didn't know enough to hide in time.

"See that," says Calac, "they don't even say thanks."

"And let's not mention the possibility of an invitation to lunch," says Polanco, who now has the bottle in hand.

"With their other visitors they bend over backwards, but with us it's the cold war. Do they think we don't know they've already had two visits?"

"As if that weren't enough, they were Swiss, if you get my drift."

"You," Calac rebukes me, "must have several secret accounts in Geneva, like all those *boom* guys, and I'm sure those who came to visit you were actually brokers bringing the latest valuations from the stock market so you can better invest your platinum ingots and things like that."

"Poor little Carol probably doesn't know anything about it," says Polanco, who's a specialist in causing rifts, "and thinks they're pure Helvetian coincidences."

And by this point we just let them talk, which deep down is what they like, and tell ourselves that in the field of coincidences, that double visit wasn't at all bad. Yesterday's was Nicole Adoum, who completely naturally told us she had to go to the dentist (in other words, from Paris to some place in Switzerland), and in view of that decided to buy some cherries and look for us in all the rest stops, which is why her little car spent three hours going on and off the autoroute like a needle sewing a seam, to the probable stupefaction of those who correctly associate the notion of a rest stop with

There are those who can appreciate the oases.

El Lobo concentrates before recording the day's scientific observations.

stopping. We loved the visit and the cherries, among other things because it took us back for a moment to Paris still almost visible in the distance, and at the same time demonstrated the irrevocable reality of an expedition that at times, we have to admit, tends to seem perfectly absurd.

(But as for absurdity, consult Tertullian.)

That the second visitor should also have been Swiss – for people with almost no acquaintances of that nationality – seemed to us the best sign that the expedition was well aligned and protected, that our *Narren Schiff* obeyed little-understood signals and winds but was propelled just as we'd hoped: sea of surprises, coastline of wonders, upside down constellations, impromptu Swiss people, and cherries in addition to our predetermined menu.

We happened to be reading beside Fafner, beneath trees full of birds who laughed at ecology and seemed delightfully happy such a short distance from gasoline fumes and the din of the expressway; Carol, absorbed in *The Invisible Man*, by Ralph Ellison, and I trembling with horror at each new episode in Anne Rice's *Interview with the Vampire*. Suddenly a solid, smiling man finished some feverish manoeuvring in reverse that left him a few metres from our refuge, and came towards us with a "Julio, Julio!" of the kind that provokes immediate and violent crises of jealousy in Calac and Polanco, which explains their later ironic references. Incredulously I recognized René Caloz, a Swiss friend with whom I once shared the uneasy task of putting together *Correo de la UNESCO*, a magazine that looks quite simple to its subscribers, but whose political balance, to give it a decent name, meant weeks of complicated negotiations, kickings and screamings, group or individual strategies, pow-wows with the English, the Soviets, the French, Mexicans, Argentines, Icelanders, Americans, so that finally the issue would reflect in a balanced way the impartial and international spirit of UNESCO, although after the endless alchemy, purgatives, distillations, re-writings and semantic adjustments, the result tended to be rather insipid, I have to say with every affection.

Carol and René meet, we sit down in the shade, and what had seemed to

Sometimes Fafner becomes solemn, almost monumental.

With all his sails unfurled, Fafner thinks he's Paolo Uccello's dragon, and no one dares approach.

me pure coincidence turns out to be a second-grade coincidence, in other words the figure turned triangular and therefore even more fascinating. We learned that Brian Featherstone, who had visited us the night before our departure and who was up to speed on the expedition, was staying with René, and had told him about the grand project. René and I hadn't seen each other for at least six years and I'll never understand why he suddenly had such an urge to find us on the autoroute, which he had to take on his way to his house in le Gard. We could have met a hundred times in Paris, but that's what cronopios are like, and suddenly René felt like going into every single rest area one after the other until he found us (just like Nicole, from which you can deduce that the Swiss share a way of thinking that earns my respect). Was he moved by the mysterious but perceptible prestige of the expedition? Or nostalgia for a friendship that we both neglected in normal, pedestrian circumstances?

But this was not the time to worry René with problems of this sort, we were too pleased to find each other in this way, like a little miracle of affection, and I think the three of us felt at the same time that this meeting was an enrichment of the game, we in ours and René adding a bit of embroidery to his race down the freeway until finding us in one of the loops of the design.

We laughed a lot, remembering old times, when René, who was a formidable mountain climber, would return from his holidays and show me photos of himself scaling a vertical cliff face, with tiny little Swiss chalets down below looking like dominoes, and I who suffer from vertigo just looking up at the ceiling of my house would turn steadily greener and ask him to put them away before I threw up all over the office. René would put them away and then start to describe how it wasn't so terrible, but the technical details forced me to imagine myself in his position and that was even worse, so the subject of mountaineering began to be little mentioned in the conversations at the *Correo*.

Passionate about everything vertical and ascending, René was generous enough to praise our rather horizontal and crawling endeavour. When he left he gave us two bottles of *fendant* wine, that agreeable gold liquid that now, after his departure, we're drinking to him and, as they say, with him. Cherries and *fendant* . . . No one brought poor Columbus such things in the first days of *his* voyage.

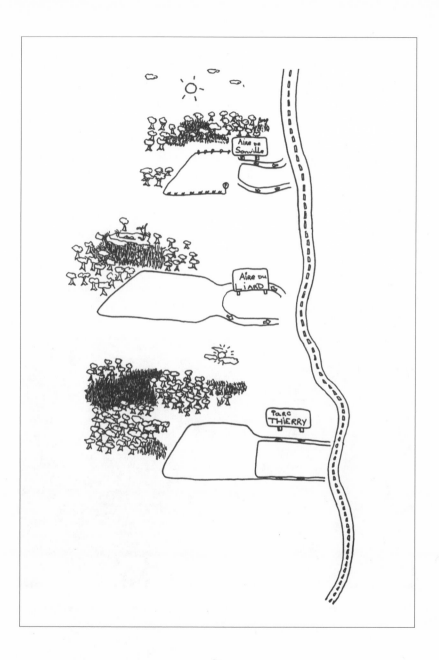

By the third day, it has become increasingly evident: out of every ten tourists driving towards the Midi, seven are British. It becomes almost boring to look at the plates, GB dominates by a long shot. (Of course, there are lots of French, but we tend to think of tourists as foreigners, and we pretend that here the French are only travelling salesmen or salesmen travelling, it doesn't matter.)

Carol admits that on our previous trips down the autoroute, the Belgians ruled in the rest areas almost offensively, while now their solitary B only peeks out from time to time. We think about the rhythms of vacations,

The Garden of Temptation, with a coded message (blue rag). Did the Company think us so desperate we'd fall into the trap of running away?

We look ahead, but the dragon's big eyes keep watch over our stern and protect us.

staggered migrations, which undoubtedly account for this British invasion, otherwise simultaneous to the one in the Malvinas Islands, the vagaries of which we follow every three or four hours by short-wave radio. I am not going to concern myself here with the Malvinas; as the Bible says somewhere, everything has its time and its place. I'll limit myself to wondering whether so many English cars on the autoroute might not be a perfectly British way for many of them to give Maggie Thatcher the finger and trade the penguins of Port Stanley for the roulette wheel of Monte Carlo.

<u>Breakfast: oranges, madeleines, fig jam, coffee.</u>

9:36 Departure.

9:38 Enter Département du Loiret.

9:46 Stop: AIRE DE PARC THIERRY.

Largest rest area we've seen so far.

Fafner facing: E.

Return of Siberian cold spell.

<u>Lunch: spaghetti with homemade sauce, cherries,
coffee.</u>

18:30 Departure beneath a timid sun.

18:35 Enter the Département de l'Yonne.

18:45 Stop: AIRE DES CHATAIGNERS.

Forest, wooded trails for cars.

Fafner facing: S.S.W.

<u>Dinner: poached eggs, cheese, coffee.</u>

Violent rain during the night, but Fafner withstands it
valiantly. There are two other dragons in the rest area,
at respectful distances.

Naked all of a sudden. Having bent over so abruptly that the front curtain just drops, improvised as it was at that moment with a bath towel to isolate us from the front seat that opens its vast windshield to any exterior gaze.

But what does it really matter, beneath the inconceivable quivering you transmit to my body you could have – I cry out yes, no – take me like this, with all the curtains open and a mess of blue jeans t-shirts bundles books and cars that keep passing in the distance and nearby too, if you'd had enough room to do it. Drunk on your body, the rest is no more than abstraction.

Do you think one day I'll figure out that way I had of closing the front curtain in a fraction of a second again? (When there's not the slightest place to fasten anything, not even a handkerchief?)

Gardeners

According to the official map of the autoroute, in this rest area there's nothing, it's just a "*zone du repos*". As soon as we install ourselves, we discover that not only do travellers occupy it for brief pauses to have a picnic or a washroom break, but a more stable population stirs in its territory, engaged in redesigning and expanding it. Young workers are finishing flowerbeds with fresh soil, and as we set Fafner up beside a propitious little woodland, we see two of them repeating the bucolic gesture of scattering seeds for what we suppose will be a future lawn. Later another worker arrives to lift the stones the plow left exposed; with slow movements full of an ancient grace, he bends to pick up the stones, gathers them in a sure armful, and goes to throw them onto a pile that grows little by little. From my vantage point – a shaded stone table where we savoured a fragrant salad of chickpeas and onions prepared by Carol for lunch – I watch this scene at once outside of time and merged with the vertiginous pace of cars and trucks on the freeway barely hidden by a grassy bank.

Ever more immersed in this interregnum where things and times diffuse, confuse and sometimes fuse, what relation persists between that race where only the yet-to-be-reached counts, the *beyond* that concentrates and petrifies the gaze of drivers, and this eternal theme of spring and germination, this gesture outside of history with which the young workers throw handfuls of seeds to the earth?

M*UTATION*

As usual, practice sends all overconfident theory to hell. It was predictable that an advance along a freeway where everyone travels at maximum velocity, stopping only to empty their bladders, fill their gas tanks, or at most to stretch their legs in a friendly rest area, would be very different from the perspective of this imperceptible crawling in which everything is reversed: the vehicle loses its importance since almost as soon as it leaves a rest area it has to drop anchor in the next; urinary or intestinal urgencies are no longer a reason to change course or interrupt the planned itinerary; the rest areas

Mini-campsite in a hostile zone: Fafner-wall, the Florid Horrors, tiny table and jerry can of drinking water.

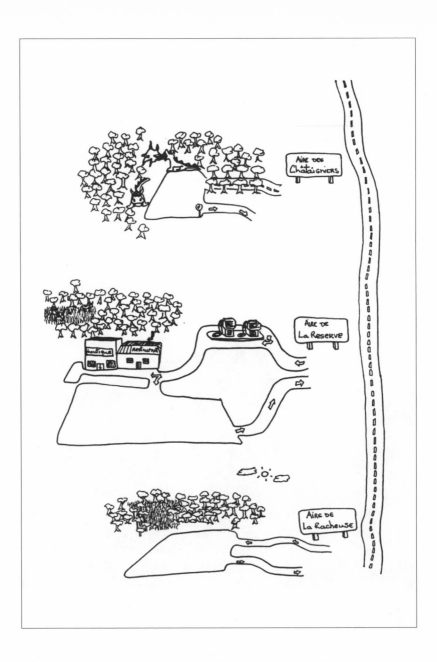

become infinitely more important than the white ribbon laid out in a space that devours the motorist who is devouring it.

All these alterations were foreseeable while we were preparing for the expedition, but no theoretical anticipation could have given us an idea of their magnitude, their riches. We're barely into the third day of the trip and the usual parameters have yielded to another way to live the freeway. Initial sensations: just beyond Fontainebleau, we have the impression of being very far away from Paris, to such an extent that Marseille doesn't seem any farther away than our point of departure. Time bites into space, transforms it; we cannot yet imagine any important differences between this rest area and the last ones that await us towards the end of the expedition.

Even more important: the gradual alteration of the usual notion of the freeway, the substitution of its insipid and almost abstract functionality by a presence full of life and riches: the people, the stops, the episodes in their more or less wooded settings, successive acts of a play that fascinate us and for which we're the only audience. Fafner, red dragon, devourer of kilometres over so many years and countries, is now a docile, immobile elephant who only moves for ten or twenty minutes a day to stay again placidly anchored on his four rubbery feet. He doesn't take it badly, quite the contrary, he seems to be in solidarity with us and his orange roof, which we raise at every stop and which turns him into a little house where it's pleasant to live, read and write, is like a sign that he's fluffing himself up, satisfied to be giving us the best of himself. We haven't the slightest doubt that Fafner is the third explorer and that he approves of this advance in slowness and profundity, while he might have considered other journeys too frivolous, too much slackening of the reins, which does not unduly please dragons or elephants.

Second metamorphosis: the freeway users. What idea did we have of that fauna launched at full speed, barely broken for a sandwich or a run to the washroom? Of course, when it comes to tedium after fifty or eighty equally monotonous kilometres, the only possible subjects of conversation arise: "Look, another Belgian, that makes five now. There's a German, four

French, two Swiss and one English. And that plate? Looks like Bulgaria. Bulgaria, how strange, first time I've seen a Bulgarian around here." And the trucks: "They're getting bigger all the time, and scarier, they go at a hundred or a hundred and ten an hour now, they've got no respect, and those articulated ones that suddenly turn into snakes and swipe you with their tail, you have to keep well away from them when you pass, but usually it's them who pass you, they really drive like lunatics."

None of that has changed deep down, but it's all changed for us. Observations en route have gone down to zero or not much more: everything now happens at the rest areas, where trucks and cars enter slowly, almost delicately, to stop very carefully next to each other. What was an enormous threatening parallelepiped, a racing car called Porsche or a zigzagging Renault 5, approach us now with the slow and friendly wiggling of a dog in search of petting or a cat who suspects leftover sardines.

But that's minor next to the essential: *things* look for their places, stop, and from the things begin to descend *human beings*, only theoretically presumed in the implacable freeway race. From that enormous truck that announces itself as TRANSPORTS VIALLE, with headquarters in Thiviers, Périgord, and which had passed us like a horrendous blue and white dinosaur at a hundred kilometres an hour, terrifying the pacific Fafner, now descends a blond boy who stretches his legs beside the door, waves in a friendly way when he sees us so close, and walks off cheerfully towards the snack bar where a relaxing steak-frites and red wine await him. From the overbearing Mercedes that undoubtedly never leaves the fast lane emerges a couple that the car seems to eject at the same time from its two front doors, like a strange mutant hen able to lay two eggs with distinct Germanic appearances at once. The *things*, then, really are inhabited; the rest areas are the place and time of truth, where life still has two legs and two arms, while the robots of the freeway lie still, dispirited, dead in their silence and powerlessness.

Breakfast: oranges, madeleines, fig jam, coffee.

10:08 Departure. Fog.

10:15 Stop: AIRE DE LA RESERVE. Cows!

First things first: we give Fafner a drink (regular gasoline, since he is a dragon of simple tastes).

Grey weather, with sunny breaks. Not as cold as yesterday. There's a shop and a restaurant. We buy a thermometer to replace the one that doesn't work.

Fafner facing: S.E.

Lunch: eggs with mayonnaise, steak-frites, chocolate mousse, coffee (in the restaurant).

13:10 First telephonic contact with rescue patrol; all well in Paris.

13:18 Departure.

13:21 Enter Burgundy.

13:24 Stop: AIRE DE LA RACHEUSE.

Lovely wooded rest area.

20°C.

We find a caterpillar.

Dinner: sauerkraut (which gives us nightmares), cheese, coffee.

Scientific observations: At the second rest area we observed a terracotta-coloured slug, who put its head into an empty beer bottle on the ground. In the evening, after having parked Fafner prudently on a patch of land free of impurities, we cook some sauerkraut.

Immediately afterwards we observe the presence of a slug, also brick-coloured, which is approaching our vehicle. Five minutes later, the whole surface of the ground in front of Fafner is covered in slugs advancing towards our

dinner. Considering the incident of the second rest area
in light of this evening's experience, we reach the
conclusion that slugs are of German origin.
(Find images of slugs, their Latin name, etc.) Are they a
sign of enemy presence? Don't forget the cork carefully
stuck on the wire.

LETTERS FROM A MOTHER (II)

Savigny-sur-Orge, 31 May, 1982

My dear son,

Thank you very much for the postcard. How do you manage to get around in a country where there's so much snow? Did you get the parcel with the wool socks and the scarf? I'd like to know whether you're allowed to wear red socks during military service, since I've got enough wool left over from the scarf to knit you another pair, but I wonder if maybe it's against regulations.

Here time goes by slowly, there's not much on television. Now that the windows are open because it's so hot, we realize that there really are a lot of children in this neighbourhood, and they annoy your father at siesta time. I wonder if we were right to sell the shop and the house, really we could have kept going for a few more years, I think, but maybe you're right and we should be free to make the most of the time we've got left, but I can tell you we're still not really used to what they now call leisure. Of course, it's very nice to think we can pick up and go whenever we feel like it, any day of the week, but in general we'd rather Sunday fell on a Sunday. When we try a Tuesday or a Thursday, it's not the same.

I don't think your father is seriously thinking of going back into business – his back troubles him too much for that – but he keeps looking at the ads, and to begin with last week we went to Joigny where they've had to put Aunt Héloïse in a home, poor thing, and then to Auxerre where your father had heard about a bar being sold for an attractive price. I wasn't too crazy about the bar idea, but the ad mentioned a cottage with a garden, and sometimes I think if I had a garden, time would pass more quickly. In any case, we left early Friday morning, and stopped in Joigny to pick up poor Héloïse's things. If you'd seen the state of the house you would have felt terrible. I did what I could to tidy up a bit but your father was thinking mostly of the bar, of course, although I imagine with that type of business we'd see your cousin

André arriving every evening after work, even if he lived far away. For twenty years his father's been spending time in the cafés, and I'm very much afraid the poor lad has already taken the same path. Your father was in a hurry to get going, so I couldn't do as much as I wanted. We went back onto the autoroute and as usual your father realized we didn't have enough gasoline, so we stopped at one of those super-stations, which I think he prefers, there are more cars than at normal service stations and they sell all sorts of things for cars besides. There are times when I think your father would have been happier as a mechanic than as a merchant, but it's too late now and I don't think I personally could have put up with a man who smelled like grease every day. In any case, when I saw your father had got them to open the hood and was chatting with a young mechanic, I got out of the car and at that moment I was in for a surprise. In the rest area was the same couple (remember I told you about that couple with the little house-on-wheels in my last letter), only last time they were near Ury and a week's gone by since then. It might be that they travel a lot around here, but you won't deny it was a strange coincidence. We, who travel on the autoroute so frequently, practically never meet the same mechanics in the service stations. And as if that weren't enough, they'd taken out two deckchairs and a little table, as if they were about to have a picnic. Anyway, they didn't see me this time, I got back in the car and we carried on to Joigny. After making sure Aunt Héloïse was all settled in – there was nothing more we could do, the poor dear didn't even recognize us – we went to have lunch in a restaurant before coming back. Your father, stubborn as ever, insisted on eating sauerkraut in spite of the heat and the fact that he still had to drive for quite a while. I told him again and again it was too heavy, but you know how he listens to me, it's just like talking to a deaf man who doesn't know how to lip-read. Thank goodness he didn't drink too much . . . (You, now that you're qualified, could you tell me what it is that drives men to drink? Your father's never lacked for anything, as far as I know.)

But in any case, sauerkraut is sauerkraut, and the result was that as soon as we got back onto the autoroute, we had to stop at the first rest area we came to so he could digest it properly. For once, you know how your father always travels with one eye on the clock, remember the trips we used to take when you were little, it was even difficult to get him to stop when you had to go pee-pee, my poor little angel. Well, for once it wasn't a service station but what they call a rest stop, with trees, paths through the woods, and surprisingly clean sanitary facilities. Your father fell asleep and I went for a walk. With the life we lead, as you well know, one has to look for pleasant moments whenever possible, and my fondest hope is that your life might be different. Of course, as you know, I've nothing to complain about. Anyway, since the other day we couldn't go to Fontainebleau on account of your cousin André and the tennis, I decided to go for a walk along the paths that went into the woods. And I had to rub my eyes there, because that same couple I'd already seen twice was installed at the back of the rest area, and not only had they got out their deckchairs and little table but they'd also set up two typewriters and both of them were writing, there in the woods. Can you imagine? When he saw me passing by, the man smiled and said "Good afternoon, madame," as if we'd run into each other in the bakery each with a loaf of bread in hand. The woman looked up and smiled at me as well. Can you make heads or tails of this? They're not that young, and it's obvious that with the vehicle they have they could find more appropriate places to work, don't you think? Anyway, I thought it was a shame you weren't with me, you would undoubtedly have found a way to speak to them.

Just as was to be expected, the bar was nothing like it sounded in the advertisement, and the garden, if you can call a piece of wasteland covered in garbage and pasture a garden, was right up against the railway tracks, so we made that whole journey for nothing. But we've decided to take a little vacation next week, your father's promised me. Maybe we'll go somewhere over near Dijon, and he's sworn to me that it won't be anything to do with business.

I know these things bother you, at your age, with the diplomas you have and all; but I confess that since you left I feel an emptiness in my life. It's only two years, your father tells me, and he also tells me I should let you live your life, and I suppose he's right. But I would have rather had you closer while you were doing your military service. You never know what's going to happen in this life, and Canada is far away, no matter how you look at it.

Well, I'll leave you. Anne-Marie telephoned a little while ago, it seems there's a good clearance sale on at Cécile's.

You know we think of you often, and send all our love,

Maman

(to be continued)

At the Racheuse rest area, a friendly caterpillar demonstrates that we are not the only explorers in these parts.

Frugality does not rule out fantasy at lunchtime in l'Aire de la Biche.

I put the deckchair in the shade of a pine tree to read the paper; the shade went away and the sun arrived, but I didn't realize until I woke up from a long, sweet and now almost forgotten dream, I only know there were wolves and maybe a train.

The feeling one so often has upon waking in a bed, in a room not in your house, when you're not surrounded by your usual walls and you might say the unconscious always takes a while to redecorate; not knowing where you are but already, before opening your eyes, the impression of difference, even stronger this time when the ear, which maybe never sleeps (it's at least true that its function is often incorporated into dreams) sends signals saying what the fuck is that noise, not of the city nor of the country, and I open my eyes and I'm still beside the pine tree, now in the sun, and a few metres away is Fafner, handsome and faithful as ever, his door open. He's empty, Julio has stopped writing; in search of shade more than anything I enter the dragon, eat some of Nicole's cherries (me who never eats cherries, since learning in the university cafeterias in Aix-en-Provence that they're almost always inhabited, I know these won't have any worms) and suddenly I realize how strange it is, when Julio doesn't return, not to know where he is . . . And the fantasy turns pleasant, he's walking around out there, he's sleeping in the grass, he's found a secret path. And I make up another game, Julio has no idea where I'm seeing him walk, the things he does, and I'm not going to tell him either because there's good and bad, the usual problem: when you open the door to the fantastic, you go all the way in, and I'm surprised to suddenly see Julio walking along with his usual smile, says he's had a great time sunbathing, took off all his clothes except his shorts in a field, and then I think: while you were pulling off your sweater you were walking along that path, at the moment you took off your jeans you'd climbed a tree and were looking at what was on the other side of the hills, not to mention that when you put your shirt on the bench beside you . . . , but I'm not going to tell you about the men who came or the city, all that was also born of your freedom or that of dreams.

To the reader:

This text of Carol's seems to be cut off here, or perhaps a page got lost; Julio did nothing more than correct the odd mistake, leaving her all her freedom and even the odd naughty word, which Carol uses with the ease of all foreigners who handle a language not their own (when they're not a stupid puritan).

Significantly, la Osita used Spanish again later to talk about Calac and Polanco, who sort of out of habit (bad habit, say some) Julio tends to introduce in his novels and other texts, under the pretext that it's them, wretched Tartars, who barge in on their own. I know that just like the diabolical "company" that holds us hostage, Carol takes very seriously the occasional invasion of my two pals who pretend to protect us and in the meantime drink our wine and eat our pâté, when we've barely got enough for ourselves. Since I'm a bit bored of them, I'm thrilled that she's the one who makes them appear a couple of times before tiring of them in her turn as was to be expected. You can tell that deep down she's become fond of them, which is a relief since the two Tartars are one of my most reprehensible weaknesses.

7:15   Beautiful morning. 12°C.

   Breakfast: orange juice, madeleines, fig jam, coffee.

8:09   Departure.

8:11   Auxerre landscapes in the morning mist. Auxerre
   itself visible in the distance.

8:26   Stop: AIRE DE LA BICHE.

Another "three star" rest area.

15°C.

Fafner facing: W.

12:00   20°C. Marvelous sunshine.

   Lunch: *mousse d'oie aux cèpes*, tinned vegetables,
   vanilla custard, coffee.

Several airplanes fly over us at low altitude, the "company"? Another sign: the branch of a dry pine fixed in the
perimeter fence.

17:10   Pause on the way out of parking area to replenish
   drinking water supply.

17:15   Departure. 24°C.

17:19   Cross Yonne River.

17:22   Stop: AIRE DES BOIS IMPERIAUX.

   22°C. Fafner facing: S.

18:45   Facing an invasion of "caravans" (in this still,
   empty rest stop, two cars pulling said "caravans" install
   themselves right next to Fafner), we decamp to the far
   side.

   Dinner: chicken soup, sweet and sour pork, cheese,
   pears, coffee.

Scientific observations: Mosquitoes going into action
(is this not proof that we're making progress?).

Fortunately, before departure, Catherine Lecuillier

provided us with a super-scientific and super-efficient
weapon against said beasts. We take it out of its case and
hear a slight buzzing that puts the mosquitoes to flight
but leaves us with a rather sad idea of their sex lives.
In effect, the machine produces a sound identical to that
emitted by the male mosquito (in rut, if such a thing is
conceivable in a mosquito), resulting in all the female
mosquitoes beating a hasty retreat (it seems they're the
ones who bite). But then, how do they reproduce?

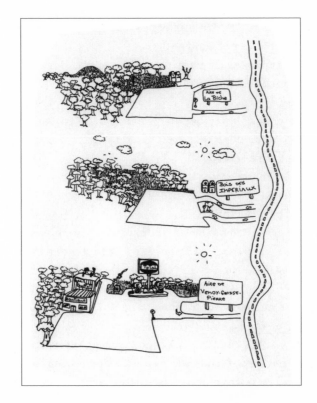

PROGRESSIVE ENTRY INTO THE OTHER.
– CONSIDERATIONS ON GARBAGE CANS
– SIOUX AND COMANCHES ON THE FREEWAY

We could never have imagined, and we have to admit – with much rejoicing – that though imagination had helped us to invent and prepare for the expedition, it had failed utterly to give us the slightest inkling of what was really going to happen. That by the middle of the trip we'd have fallen into step, even a routine, was to be expected, but that by the fifth day, and barely at the gates of Burgundy, we should be leading a life that can only be defined as *natural*, stuns us at times.

All the rest is almost parenthetical, although the radio and newspapers we find every once in a while keep us up to date on wars, film festivals, murders, book reviews and labour disputes. All that is, all that goes on; but it is and goes on in the no man's land of two rest stops per day, of two islands that Fafner reaches after a few insignificant minutes of insignificant progression. Maybe that's the strangest part: what should have been the fundamental thing, travelling slowly down the Autoroute du Sud, lost all importance from the very first day. The symptoms of the freeway – monotony, obsessive time and space, fatigue – do not exist for us; as soon as we get on it we get off again and forget it for five, ten hours, all night long. What can it matter to us if we barely see it, segmented as it will be in more than sixty pieces, brochette of serpent instead of a whole and hissing snake?

Nature on the other hand doesn't cause the least feeling or fear of monotony. Rest stops are what they are, poor little darlings, but each one represents an interesting modification within the basic outline. When we find a good place to stop Fafner, looking for the shade of a woods or in the worst case a place as far as possible from the noise of the freeway, each time we discover the alteration of the common elements. The washrooms that were ten metres to our right are now twenty to the left or behind us; last night's little woods of svelte trunks is now a mass of oaks from which hang here and there cute little caterpillars who crawl across our jeans or typewriters, and who look at us (that is definitely true, they look at us and seem happy and confident as if they knew we were going to play with them awhile and then put them on a big leaf so they stop bothering us); the tables and benches of rustic boards, where it's so pleasant to have lunch or dinner, are laid out in different ways, just like the garbage cans, whose generous abundance overwhelms us.*

All this doesn't really register on a quick trip, when the rest areas are just hygienic or gastronomical breaks; no one is going to start making detailed comparisons with the previous rest area since, with apologies for the auto-paraphrase, *all Aires the Aire*. But our case is very different: we've barely emerged from one when we're already anticipating the next, conjecturing about its possible qualities or fearing a nasty surprise, modelling according to our desires the next refuge, which a few minutes later will show its first big P and its promise of arriving in 1,000 metres, then 200, and then again the ritual of pulling in slowly, studying the possibilities, discarding false advantages experience has already revealed. This afternoon, for example, the best place under some golden and shady oaks was taken by a large family who had organized lunch at one of the tables and was enjoying it as was right and proper. Similar to Sioux warriors, to stealthy Comanches, we

---

* On a scientific level we should point out that this abundance, obviously unsightly but destined to shame anyone who still thinks empty cans and dirty wrappers are meant to carpet the ground, sometimes strikes us as excessive. We go so far as to imagine that the Authority in charge of public highways ordered a certain number of trash cans, that a distracted secretary added two zeroes, and finding they couldn't rectify the error opted for "better too many than not enough". That's why you can almost throw your garbage away with your eyes closed, especially between Paris and Lyon; beyond that the model changes (another careless secretary?) and they get smaller and a little anthropomorphic, somewhere between a robot and the Teutonic knights in Aleksandr Nevsky, but they proliferate all over the place just the same.

Projected tourist poster for Parkingland (Aire de la Biche).

A tropical woodland near Auxerre (Aire de la Biche).

stopped Fafner fifteen metres away with the look of people just stopping to have a drink or stretch our legs, but while Carol, like Princess Pocahontas lying in wait for palefaces, walked around in a blasé manner, calculating exactly when the family might go from coffee to car, I stayed alert behind the wheel so that German or Parisian tourists wouldn't dart in like a flash and take our spot.

These slightly surreptitious manoeuvres will seem ingenuous but they're not. We could absolutely not tell those who want to deprive us of the spot that we're going to be living on the autoroute for thirty-three days, because they'll immediately think about the necessity of phoning a psychiatrist, or at least, the police. And nevertheless, being comfortable is of prime importance to those who have to face so many weeks of an arduous expedition; at risk is their health, their good moods, this book and its readers, and such excellent reasons justify our prowling, crouching in wait if necessary, and any other legitimate way to set ourselves up as we like. Weren't cities created in this way, and even nations? Rivers, coasts and convenient heights, appropriate climates: one doesn't pitch one's tent in any old spot, as Romulus and Remus will tell you, as will Niemeyer or Pedro de Mendoza.

The first drops of rain brush the snail's delicate antennae and he rapidly shuts himself up in his little spiral house. In less than a minute we've folded the deck chairs (alias the Florid Horrors on account of the pattern on the fabric, which Carol in her perversity didn't want to change in spite of my pleas) and taken refuge inside Fafner who a few moments later becomes a shiny red bubble, as undoubtedly happens to all dragons when they get caught in a downpour outside their caves.

Nothing daunts our fine explorers: la Osita sets up her typewriter on the driver's seat and sits on the passenger seat to write; in the back, I pull out the table and set up my office as befits a member of the "intelligentsia" who is also a comfort-lover and always takes the best places. Half a bottle of red and luminous burgundy accompanied by salted almonds puts us in a state similar to satori, and Fafner vibrates to the rhythm of two Olympia Traveller de Luxes, while outside a spring storm rages Byronically and visibility, as the shipping forecasts put it, becomes a likely story.

Speaking of radio, this expedition is not at all escapist. If only it were, murmurs the small perverse side of our double heart, feeling that we absolutely would never want to escape from things that probably deserve it but in which we carry on believing. The radio occupies an important place in the Paris–Marseille journey; after much reflection, we decided that of the three transistors we have at home, we'd bring the JVC (purchased from The Good Guys, San Francisco, after spending several days looking for a better short wave receiver), since it can not only connect us to local FM stations, but also gives us the most unexpected surprises: Yugoslavian, Tunisian, Danish stations and what matters most these days, the BBC World Service from London that brings us their version of what they call the Falklands War, hour after hour. And from that war, you'll have understood by now, we do not wish to, nor could we escape.

When you read this page, this afternoon's news will be a tiny slice of the immense orange of time, so many things will have happened and, as Jean Sablon used to sing in the old days:

> *Tout passe, tout casse, tout lasse,*
> *Un autre aura ma place . . .*

another war will rage on other horizons, etc., but today it's this one and it's ours, it's Latin America. How can we not be filled with anguish before the sinister pantomime of a military junta that, knowing itself reviled by the civilian population, opts for a desperate gambit and launches on the reconquest of the Malvinas, knowing full well that it means sending thousands of poorly trained and equipped conscripts to their deaths? How can we not feel sick at the stupid support of a majority of Argentines who for the last decade have experienced oppression, murder, torture and the disappearance of thousands of compatriots day after day?

(End of 19:00 bulletin. Next at 20:00.)

On the Entomological Fauna at Rest Areas and Other Ecological Considerations, as Well as the (Scant) Possibilities of Establishing a Cartography of the Arborescent Flora

Reality is quite Euclidian, and every day this expedition demonstrates its tendency to present itself in figures, which despite their intangibility insist on repeating themselves over and over again; so, as soon as the sun delivers its first Bjorn Borgian serve and plants its big yellow ball in the middle of the rest area, we run in search of shade, and the heat–tree–traveller triangle closes once again here, just as it'll be closing on so many other points of this vast sphere.

Within that triangle, we proceed to set up the Florid Horrors and allow ourselves to be enveloped in shade that filters through golden spots, sounds of leaves and birds as astute and Euclidian as we are. In general, it's not the moment for working, or it is but it can wait, which is why we feel ourselves living with that intensity that can only come from the feeling of doing nothing, an increasingly unknown sensation in daily life, the consequences of which experts pour into a brief but ominous word: stress. In our triangle there is not the slightest danger of that, we have enough in Paris where it'll be waiting for us crouching behind the door. Here it's all heat, shade and tree, a slow still navigation in the green water of the vegetal aquarium.

This afternoon's tree has no name, like most of my trees; I've never learned to distinguish more than three or four, weeping willow, poplar, plane, oak and that's about it. Not too tall but wide, it throws out its five or six stories of large branches and fluffs up into a vast crown barely discernible from my seat at the foot of its trunk. The breeze moves its broad leaves; it feels alone in its individuality, quite self-sufficient. But it's not alone, I learn gradually, and my first lesson comes from a tickle on my nose where a little caterpillar has just landed, having descended from some leaf on its silk ladder for reasons which escape me. As soon as I've cut the silk thread and put him on the ground so he can go annoy someone else, I see many little caterpillars embarked on the same operation that looks somewhat angelic, their almost imperceptible ladders letting them descend from tree to ground; a cycle has begun, a metamorphosis approaches, the little caterpillars abandon their green heaven to risk their lives on the earthly adventure that awaits them below. At the same time, the trunk, I now discover when I look more closely, is like an Yggdrasil on which strange passages take place between the high and the low; on one side a line of big black ants climbs up to disappear along the first branch on the left, while another, less disciplined line descends after a trip that doesn't appear to have afforded any provisions, unless they'd eaten them where they found them. And what intention guides this blue beetle who advances in a slow spiral like a Buddhist monk on the path to revelation? He disappears behind the trunk to reappear a few centimetres higher; at this pace he'll arrive at the top in two hours and perhaps find illumination. A dragonfly has just discovered an enthralling game: she leaves the open air to dart among the foliage, overcoming obstacles, veering off to one side and then the other while she goes up and down through the levels of the leaves, amusing herself by multiplying an itinerary that seems to have no other purpose than to make sure she never errs in her distance calculations.

Just this tree? It's taken me ten minutes to discover that it's like a universe, vibrant with lives, just as it took la Osita one second to make her shriek coincide with the ant bite somewhere on her left leg, an event that tears us out of our meditation and the Florid Horrors, and has no major consequences apart from expletives and laughter. But la Osita is worried about an

Being able to read a whole book without anyone interrupting us . . .

important problem: *Why* did the ant bite her? A pertinent question, since it's obvious that no one bothered the bug on his journey across the exposed calf, and then suddenly, for deep-seated and unknown reasons, he stopped and dug his pincers into her skin.

I realize now that we're talking about it that the ant invasion has made substantial progress on my person, and I get rid of them without awaiting their personal decisions. We haven't finished with the subject when we see an enormous army of slugs advancing across the dampest and darkest patch of ground. We admire their terracotta colour, at the same time as our incurable anthropomorphism leads us to classify them as repugnant, disgusting, slimy and other equally unjust epithets. Actually, they're very beautiful slugs, with a smooth and shiny front part followed by a dorsal section that looks like the work of Piza, our friend the Brazilian painter, I mean a surface filled with little gathers and grooves that look hand-made, although it's hard to imagine a hand working on a slug, and much less Piza's. As is their custom, this cohort of slugs advance millimetre by millimetre, giving the clear impression they're not going anywhere, except where pedestrians and vehicles will irrefutably crush them; but we're falling back into anthropomorphism, because slugs know better than us why they leave their woodland shelters and make their entrance into the rest area, although it might also be ingenuous to imagine them so sure of themselves, poor little things.

"You mustn't forget about spiders," Carol reminds me after I've consulted her regarding certain details about slugs in Canada.

"Of course, spiders . . ."

"I only mentioned them because you've got quite a big one on your shoulder."

I look at it with compassion, I who've known the tarantulas of Mendoza and the bird-eating spiders of Banfield, but I flick it away anyhow, something I'd never do to the tiny spiders who've been running over the Florid Horrors (they must like the print) and my legs since the outset. We have good relations with them and with the ladybugs and the small, furry,

Unexpected fauna in the Venoy-Grosse-Pierre rest area.

inoffensive beetles; that's not the case with flies, but there aren't that many along the autoroute, or with horseflies and wasps, the latter repelled by a pure cloud of insecticide, though ecologists condemn us.

My Florid Horror has a lever that lets me recline for a siesta; so now, seeing the tree from directly beneath it, my gaze can climb from level to level, a bit like the dragonfly, moving around in the green light that trembles slightly. This letting go is enough, this exit from oneself towards a state unattainable in a vertical position, to be the tree a little bit, live the tree and stop looking at it as usual, that-tree, that-oak or plane or chestnut; it's enough to be-in-the tree to know it in another way, if to know still means anything. Now that I come back to this certainty of plurality, of the multiform world of insects and birds (because they too play up there, passing like big black or grey or red elephants among the leaves that hide the almost invisible world of insects), I am the tree like a country of unimaginable borders, superimposing floating cities linked by a system of paths, drawbridges, moist canals of sap, landing and takeoff platforms, lakes of blue light, green pools, deserts of solar sand, closed circuits or major routes leading to the highest point, ending at the trembling frontier of the last leaves, there where the sky begins.

Cartography of the country of a tree: why not? We'd just need a series of precise photographs and the patience to flatten the spherical, like Mercator, like the makers of portolans, here's the north or the east, here's the top or the bottom, the tree's Everests and its Mediterraneans. I imagine the map of my tree, with the conventional signs, its blue and its green and its white, its hydrography, altimetry, orography and why not its ethnography (its entomology and ornithology). I imagine the cartographer drawing the tree's spherical whirl to scale on the page, showing the routes from the central shaft – the tree's freeway – spreading their bifurcations to one side and the other, splitting in their turn in two, four, fifty, two hundred, one thousand eight hundred and forty-four smaller trails, which disappear into dozens of thousands of paths, each one with its green fields, each leaf a parcel of the land registry and on each parcel an ephemeral proprietor – as all should be – the mosquito, the spider, the caterpillar, the ladybug, and even those imperceptible beings that will have names in treatises but that here, on this typewriter, every once in a while trace the infinitesimal image of a teensy creature advancing towards the keys, hesitating at the edge, retreating and disappearing at the first second of inattention, already forgotten, already nothing.

Yes, but this cartographer, would he be content with the map of a tree after weeks and weeks of work? I imagine him raising his eyes to the next one, to all the trees in the rest area, in the adjacent forests, in the country, on the continent, on Earth. I imagine him facing the task of mapping all the trees in the world, the jungles of Gabon, Amazonia, the California redwood stands, the Black Forest. Each tree a different (and ephemeral) map (but all maps are ephemeral), an individual invention of trails, intersections, passages and bridges. Unthinkable, I know, but on the other hand, what sense could there be in an atlas of the world without maps of Portugal or Venezuela?

"Let's go," Osita says to me. "You've slept for long enough, you lazy wolf."

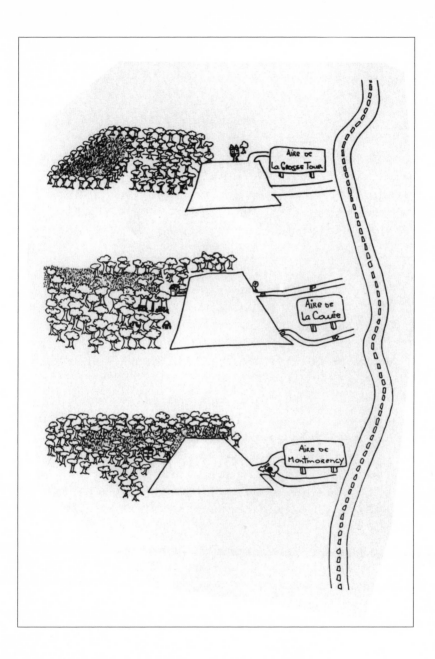

8:30   15°C
>   Breakfast: orange juice, madeleines, fig jam, coffee.

11:45   Departure. 20°C, breeze, timid sun, a bit of fog.
Uncertainty: the signs announce a hotel at the next rest
stop, but it does not appear on our map.

11:55   Stop: AIRE DE VENOY-GROSSE PIERRE.
Bar, buffet, shop, gasoline.
Fafner facing: S.E.
>   Lunch: crudités (to combat scurvy), chicken with
>   french fries, coffee (buffet "L'Arche").

13:20   Departure. The thermometer shows ... 35°C!
We buy oranges from the shop: safe from scurvy!
Second telephonic contact with the rescue patrol. Weather
misty and muggy.

13:25   Stop: AIRE DE LA GROSSE TOUR.
Tracks for vehicles. Woods, fields. Wilder rest area than
the others, beautiful. 25°C.

15:45   27°C. For the first time we notice the presence of
extremely annoying little flies, which seems to confirm
that we are indeed advancing towards the south.
>   Dinner: *mousse d'oie aux cèpes*, spaghetti (with oil or
>   butter, according to taste), coffee.
The film in the camera is finished. We'll have to draw the
remaining rest areas.

21:00   This rest area, located in the wild and tropical
verdant glade of the autoroute, is not free from danger.
During the night a merciless invasion of ferocious ants
begins. We are overrun.

Of course, we couldn't be the only ones interested in this other highway that little by little lets us in on its secrets, growing fond of us as we grow fond of it, and so with very little noise and no violence we come into possession of its trails, paths and remote places, and much like the process of gradually possessing a loved one in bed, with caresses and gazes and murmurs that

An affable slug pays a courtesy call to Fafner and his crew, who no less affably send him on his way in another direction.

bit by bit are revealed as doors and windows behind which there are always more, sweeter, lovelier, and finally no one knows who's opening which door, who is the window or who has whom in their arms. It's the same with the highway: we know that in many ways it's not at all what we used to think. Cars, trucks, ambulances pass very quickly and with a surprising gentleness, but you only have to look closely to realize that sometimes they don't have wheels and don't pass along the freeway the way a foot might pass over the ground, leaving a print behind. No, it's at once freeway, asphalt and cars, a single being that breathes and advances; sometimes one or another of its parts breaks the rhythm, leaves the main organism, and with a lateral movement carefully calculated not to break the equilibrium of the whole or injure another part of this living being that advances with the noise and cadence of a surging sea, slips out, pulls into a parking lot, and stops, and that decision – which must not always be easy because I think the living thing, which has not stopped passing in front of us for the last five days now extracts its strength from its capacity to hypnotize everyone and fix them on the freeway – is like a new creation of those that softly stop, take human form, walk, separate themselves from the machine that up till that moment *was them*.

But there's no danger for us anymore, since we've discovered up to what point the real freeway is not that, but the parallel one we've suspected for years and that we're finally experiencing (so well that it now seems perfectly normal to be here at the side of the route, we have to give our heads a shake every once in a while to remember that it's an adventure and not just another version of everyday life . . . a life already quite filled with madness for certain people, like for example those two buddies of Julio's who found out about the expedition somehow and I suppose must have got here by hitchhiking till they found us; and nevertheless, the more people used the word madness when they found out about our project, the more beauty they gave to it. They knew very well deep down that it was already too late to put us back on the straight and narrow, a road neither of us have ever taken, I don't think).

The little Michelin Man, one of the many divinities of the freeway, rules disdainfully over his faithful flock.

But of course, there are the jealous, the suspicious, those-who'd-like-to-but-would-never-have-the-courage-and-whom-nothing-would-give-greater-pleasure-than-our-failure. And there's *them* as usual: now that nothing can be heard by telephone, which has been left silent at home or ringing for no one, and who can't reach me directly with their espionage (since I don't know much about installing secret microphones, how many times have I said *Fuck you, friends*, while watering the plants or drawing the curtains, just in case), they must be furious to see that the scientific and domestic organization of the expedition is well established, and that two minutes after arriving in a rest area we're all set up, the fridge working, everything in its place and us all ready for a little coffee or something else depending on the time. Bit by bit, but very clearly, we start noticing the signs. It's obvious they're not going to intervene directly, but already on the second day of the trip, the first rest area closed, was that not a temptation for us to give up the project? Are they exasperated not to really understand what it is we're looking for? Do they perhaps believe we're plotting some suspicious meeting on the autoroute?

Maybe they don't all belong to one single organization. When the first helicopter went past, flying low over the rest area we'd just arrived at, I even thought we also had friends protecting us . . . There are various signs: the false bottle of whisky in the hotel, for example. And in front of the same hotel, when to be on the safe side we closed Fafner's curtains before going to our room, thinking that maybe sometimes he'd like a little privacy all to himself, what about that girl with the red boots who undoubtedly believed we were sleeping inside and approached to take a close-up photo? You can see they are quite misinformed since they don't even know where we are, but the fact is that the girl did take precautions and pretended she was taking a photo of a man inside the next car, but we, who were spying on her from our room, knew that to focus the viewfinder for distance you have to turn the lens towards the left, in a counter-clockwise motion, while her hand moved towards the right to take a photo of something no more than two metres away . . . Well, *no pasarán*. Basically, it's best to let them go on believing we're stupid. Oh, and the other signs: those English people, but so English that they're obviously in disguise, and who've stopped as if to repair something in their trailer. And that mysterious tent that was set up beside us sometime during the night?

More than anything else, they amuse us. If they're not ready to experience the same alchemy as us, they're never going to find the route.

"Route, toot," mocks Polanco from somewhere unseen. They're jealous, they think expeditions are for men on their own, and since as well as a woman I'm not very big, I'll have to pretend to be a frail creature and not share the whisky, which we have on rations, to leave more for them. For now they won't even show themselves, they laugh at me from behind the trees, how brave! And the freeway remains still, and people with cars pass over top of it.

"They're moving," says Calac, who's maybe getting to like me a little. "They're making tracks."

"They're moving . . . Now you'll see, they think they're philosophers, do you know why?"

"Pure pretext, this philosophizing justifies their idleness."

"All this fuss just because they feel like making love without the telephone ringing or having to keep appointments or anything."

"They never did it with the phone, *che*."

"What do you know? The scoundrels close the door."

Out of pure annoyance, because I know in a minute or two they'll start making fun of my Argentine accent (and what do you know about tangos?), I decide it's time for a drink, and there won't be any for them.

Breakfast: oranges, biscuits, coffee.

8:00 Temperature, 15°C. Cloudy.

9:15 Departure.

9:21 We've come as far as Vézelay, "Colline Eternelle".

9:27 Stop: AIRE DE LA COUÉE.

Woods, tables. Fafner facing: S.S.E.

Lunch: crabmeat sautéed with peas and onions, rice, coffee.

15:15 Flight occasioned by invasion of talkative barbarians.

15:25 Stop: AIRE DE MONTMORENCY.

25°C. Fafner facing: W.S.W.

17:30 Surprise storm. Large raindrops despite bright sunshine. We take refuge in Fafner (alas, so do the flies). The thermometer goes from 25°C to 19°C in 20 minutes. Lovely rest area.

Dinner: *bami-goreng*, coffee.

Eight days on the freeway now.

No: the freeway is precisely what's lacking, for us it's nothing more than a background noise in the distance that habit reduces day by day, that we've effortlessly likened to an agreeable echo of the Caribbean sea in Martinique or Guadeloupe. It's true, we mustn't let ourselves get carried away so mechanically by a scale of aesthetic values (the sound of the sea is a thousand times more beautiful that that of a freeway, etc.): with eyes closed, the equivalence can reach disturbing levels. Truck-waves, engine-whitecaps... In any case, there are the same intervals of silence, the approximation and crescendo of the next break, that diastole and systole of a waving, breath-

There are those who know how to travel, though they don't stray far from their vehicle.

ing, sometimes unbearable resounding volume such as we've known on Martinique's beaches and in the rest areas.

So, as seems clearer and clearer, our expedition is first and foremost a navigation of this archipelago of parking lots. We never would have believed it before, because in our memories of our usual trips it's the autoroute who rules alone. Little by little we become pleasantly convinced that our expedition is leading, like that of Columbus, towards a totally different outcome from what we expected. The Admiral was looking for the Indies and we for Marseille; he found the Antilles and we found Parkingland.

Because this is a country, whose provinces we are conquering at a rate of two per day, planting our red Fafnerian flag, drawing up the necessary cartography, taking inventory of the flora and fauna (in yesterday's rest area there was such a quantity of crows that for a moment we thought we were in a wildlife sanctuary; shortly afterwards we discovered something worse: ants, but we'll talk about that later).

For us, Parkingland is a world of liberty. If the rules of the game oblige us to explore two provinces per day, we're not going to leave the country because of that, and our duty does not deprive us of the feeling of doing whatever we feel like. The conduct of the Parkinglandians (I mean the freewayistas who spend their days or nights in the rest areas) does nothing but multiply this feeling of liberty, because it must be said, alas, that the poor things proceed in a way that, while hesitating to pour scorn on anyone, can only be classified as idiotic. One or another might carry in their heart the seed of freedom, and then we regard them with respect, we're ready to strike up a dialogue, to lend a can opener or chat about the weather and the temperature. But almost everyone comes into the parking lot looking like they have full bladders or empty stomachs, and these looks don't seem to be replacing intelligence or sensitivity. They pee, they eat (almost always standing up, almost always sandwiches) and flee as if the rest area were full of crocodiles and snakes. Do they suffer from Parkingson's disease? The only ones who are different, as ever, are the children and the dogs: they leap from the cars like multicoloured springs, run among the trees, explore the kingdom, marvel at the flowers and the lawns, until a terrible whistle or an ear-splitting "*Henri!!*" returns them sadly to the tin can, which they enter with the sadness typical of all packed sardines.

Increasingly alone as night grows nearer (we already know the waxing and waning rhythm of the Parkinglandian demography), we take advantage of the last light to walk around each new island and consolidate our compassionate conquest step by step. At some moment we arrive at the boundary, and this boundary is a high barbed-wire fence, like in concentration camps. Beyond it the forest continues, a field begins, a village is sketched against the horizon; the world carries on beyond, but we could not go towards it even if the rules of the game allowed us to. And we both feel now that for once the rules of the game have their sinister side as well, a bitter negativity. Parkingland is beautiful; it is ours, we are free within it, and we love it. But its boundary is the mirror of other boundaries that history has made horrible; it's like seeing the image of Treblinka, of Auschwitz. It does us good to return to our dragon, feel the undeserved but marvelous happiness of being on the good side of the wires, for now.

Breakfast: oranges, biscuits, coffee.

11:16 Departure filled with regret, since it was an
extraordinarily beautiful rest area.

11:22 Avallonnais landscape. (Cows on the left and the
right).

11:25 Morvan regional natural park.

11:30 Stop: AIRE DE CHAPONNE.
Gasoline, restaurant. Fafner facing: S.S.E.

Lunch: appetizer "de la maison", roquefort salad,
brochettes with prunes, ice cream (coffee and hazel-
nut), coffee.

12:55 Departure after excellent lunch at the "Gril 4
Pentes".

12:57 Roadwork, traffic reduced to a single lane.

13:00 End of roadwork and entry to Département of Côte
d'Or.
Storm threatening. Will we have time to get set up at the
next rest area before it breaks? The sky darkens like in a
Hitchcock movie.

13:02 (Barely legible note, something like "great big
naked Pan"). Cows on our right.

13:03 Stop: AIRE D'ÉPOISSES.
Fafner facing: E.
We've arrived at our first nightmare rest area: a narrow
strip of asphalt next to the freeway. Carol baptizes it
"Aire de la Poisse", in other words, Aire of Rotten Luck,
for not only are we stuck right beside the freeway, but
there's also a diabolical storm raging.
To make matters worse, it's not so much the roar of the
cars that keeps us from sleeping, but the shriek of the

high speed train that passes like a jet plane along the
viaduct right beside the parking lot.

18:06 37°C! (But in the shade, we don't feel the heat.)

Dinner: mixed salad, ham, eggs, apples, raisins.
Coffee.

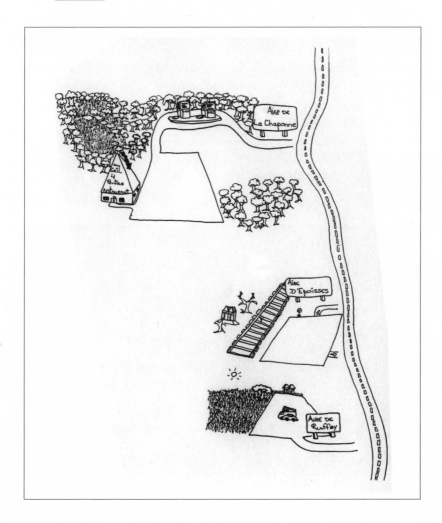

Honestly, we have to recognize that human stupidity helps us enormously on this expedition. No one has sold their jewels for our benefit, as they tell us Isabel the Catholic Queen did to give a hand to Christopher Columbus, or like those UNESCO secretaries who once went round collecting money to save the baby seals cruelly massacred by Scandinavians greedy for furs or oil. No patron handed us a blank cheque, and obviously when we arrive at the rest areas we find neither the big-hearted Englishman nor the Mexican of gentlemanly conduct who will hurry to remove their Mercedes or their Porsche to let us have the only shady spot. But we don't mind, because we are, however, the beneficiaries of a strange unwritten law, according to

Scientific observations on the effects of gas in water when mixed in a siphon.

which tourists who travel to escape from the urban hell, from the atmospheric contamination and the din of the streets, tend in their surprising majority to stop their cars as close to the freeway as possible, practically at the entrance or exit of the parking lot. Happy, relaxed, in shorts and t-shirts, they set up their tables and chairs (and radio and even television) beside their cars, in order to watch them up close just in case, you know, crime these days, look what happened in Poitiers, went for a pee and when she came back they'd broken a window and made off with the pearl necklace her father had given her as a wedding present no less!

If anyone doesn't believe us, they should go for a modest weekend outing along the roads that skirt the great forests of the Ile-de-France, Rambouillet for example. These forests are full of marvelous trails leading to zones of perfect tranquility, perfect precisely because there's no one there: the families stop their cars five metres away from the freeway, so they can get a good view of it and meanwhile relentlessly breathe in all the emanations from the tailpipes of all the other cars, and right there they set up their tables, chairs, babies and grandmothers. In the rest areas it's less glaring, people pluck up the courage to drive quite a way in and some even take up the best spaces, but statistically it's easy to verify that the majority remain integrated in a ribbon of cars as close as possible to the freeway. Carol thinks that maybe those people have a fear of wolves, atavism dies hard, and you know, in the woods . . . I, less romantic, think they're simply idiots, and thanks to that we are much helped on our valiant expedition.

CONVERSATIONS EN ROUTE

The rest areas are starting to mount up like the clear and also vague scenes of a long dream, one after the other; it's the stages of the journey and not clocks that mark time, that cancel it out, because deep down we are outside of time in the same way we're outside the freeway. Experiencing it, but it's no longer the enemy of bells, chimes, and postage stamps, it's the friend turning into a tree when we want to have a drink or read in the shade, it's that sort of non-difference between the rest areas, each one a living space, and the asphalt strip of speed seems further and further away and ever more alien. Already Fafner, as if he knew something of the project (and he is undoubtedly coming to understand the essence of the game bit by bit, each time we fold down his roof and sit up front, turning him once more into an automobile, he makes the sweetest noise, runs along during those ten or fifteen minutes on the road as if he suddenly had pillows on his tires, as if he didn't want to disturb all the everyday things we're carrying with us), integrates into the rest areas as if he were part of the camouflage, he approaches the trees, hides in the most private corners, and even flutters his yellow fringes as if they were tiny young leaves calling out to the birds.

I can understand a little why so many people would be almost frightened to make this trip. Rest areas are nothing more than emptiness with décor. You have to know how to fill them. And in spite of the geographical or physical differences, they're always the same. It will really be a surprise, I think, to see at the end that we've also advanced according to the criteria of others; I mean we'll have arrived in Marseille in spite of the immobility that characterizes us.

"Immobility *mon cou*," says Calac who'd do well to take a few French lessons, not that I could care less about his neck even though I know he means something else. "Leaving that rest area that had a restaurant and everything so quickly, just when we were about to have some *fritas*."

"Pommes *frites*," says Polanco who takes every opportunity to display his knowledge.

"Do they think it's easy to move along this damn highway without a car? Especially these days, us being Argentines and almost all the cars coming from the land of Her Majesty?"

"The worst is catching up to them afterwards, *che*. It seems like it's against the law to ask for a lift for less than fifty kilometres. They won't stop."

But I know they haven't come back on foot, the swine, they'll have crossed over some bridge after finding a car coming up the other side. They're not going to tire themselves out that much just to hassle us.

"And us coming all this way out of the goodness of our hearts! Look, they don't even notice how boring their trio must be."

I'd tell them to go to hell, but I know it'd be the pretext they're waiting for to start teasing me about how little I know about tangos.

"And you two, what do you know about Scottish ballads?"

"Ay," says Calac, touching his head as if he'd had too much to drink last night. "You're not going to start singing like last time in Burgundy?"

"There aren't any stars, *che*. They only do that under the stars."

We let them talk. It's cheap, after all.

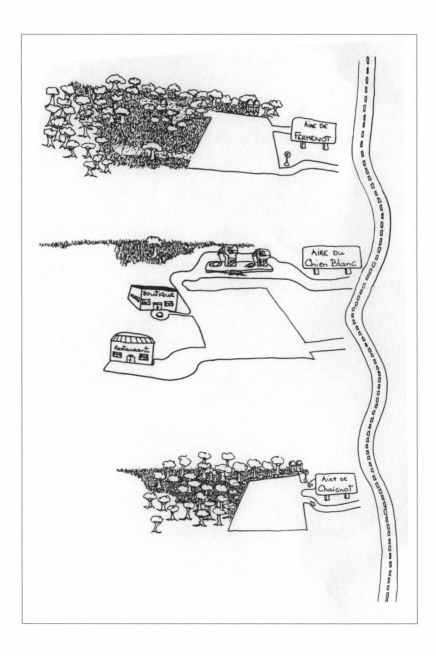

Breakfast: oranges, biscuits, fig jam, coffee.
8am 20°C.

8:18 Departure beneath a light fog.

"Burgundy: vineyards and gastronomy."

8:25 We've come as far as Sémur-en-Auxois.

8:29 Stop: AIRE DE RUFFEY.

Fafner facing: S.W.

We get set up to await the arrival of reinforcements.

12:58 Arrival of Anne and Necmi, first gastronomical, aesthetic and moral support.

Lunch: (4 courses) brochettes, haricots verts, compote . . . and a fresh baguette from Paris.

Note: All uncertainty with respect to the logistical

First logistical rendezvous: Necmi Gurmen and Anne Courcelles bring us fresh provisions and good cheer in the Ruffey rest area.

effectiveness of the expedition is pulverized by the embraces, shouts of joy and reciprocal congratulations. Or, to put it more modestly, the stowage manoeuvres of NASA's capsules pale into insignificance beside the success of such a brilliant operation. Not to mention the accompanying lunch that was nothing like that horrible vitamin paste the poor cosmonauts had to swallow after squeezing a tube; our banquet consists in aromatic red and green victuals, exquisite wines and crusty fresh bread, which adorn our table and make it tremble with emotion beneath such unusual weight.

15:10 42°C.

16:04 Farewell to our assistants, and departure.

16:14 Stop: AIRE DE FERMENET.

Even more beautiful than the Aire de Villiers rest area. Fafner facing: W.

18:46 20°C.

Dinner: *radis-beurre* with baguette. Chicken (masterpiece of Anne Courcelles), salad (with baguette), compote, coffee.

An aquarium light, as Julio calls it as he settles with a book into one of the Florid Horrors (but horrid as they may be, I'm increasingly sure this poor taste – owing not to the perversity of which he accuses me, but rather the lack of time on that vertiginous autoroute that Paris had turned into during the weeks leading up to the departure – protects us). How could the gendarmes suspect that people who unfold with total assurance such visible bad taste (we can camouflage Fafner deep in the woods, but as soon as we assemble the "salon," the lurid orange of the deck chairs can probably be seen from the previous rest area) could be anything other than honest and solid vacationers making a stop along the way, heading rapidly for one

At the sight of l'Aire du Chien-Blanc restaurant, Fafner flings open his door.

An irresistible enticement for joggers in the Fermenot rest area.

of those campgrounds that offer the innocent and noisy promiscuity of cities? Despite the typewriters, books and siestas prolonged far beyond the hours necessary to recover from the fatigues of the road, those deck chairs offer a false and different vision of our life, guaranteeing us the anonymity essential to the journey, with the freeway in the distance like a grey river and the sun setting in green puddles around Fafner.

It would be very difficult to know, if we hadn't taken the precaution of making a list of the rest areas, with the corresponding date of each, how long we've been living like this. We're ever more aware that we're conquering a territory we could call Parkingland or Liberty or even Second Home, since we've certainly found here all the advantages of the latter, though the terrain may be mobile and the neighbours nonexistent or changeable. It's a land of great silence, a land of time that lengthens and nevertheless moves on unnoticed. And little by little, if it's true that writing is an erotic experience as we've both always known it, we'll also have to start opening the pages of this book. Leave off this trial and error, make up our minds. Writing is always accepting the risk of telling all, even – and especially – unknowingly. So just as once you've accepted the adventure of love it's not a question, while the other is pulling back the sheets as if discovering a wide, warm, white beach, of saying: "Oh, but I'm not taking my underwear off", in the same way, if we've decided to truly write this book, we have to tell all (not in the sense of never shutting up, but of giving everything its freedom while writing).

There are not only demons along the way, but angels too; yesterday I met one in the WC, as if that were a place to meet angels. A poor little angel of the feminine sex, very blonde, with big round eyes that went from one Turkish-style toilet to another, while her little arms, spread like wings, held the two doors open. Hearing the exit door open behind her, she turned her head and smiled, I don't know whether because the sun streamed in as the door opened (and the wind too, for the divine perfumes that reign where angels usually float must be a bit more delicate than the smell of certain rest stop WCs), or because she saw in the human presence the solution to her dilemma. Still keeping both doors open, she looked at me while I washed my hands in an attempt to adopt a natural attitude (I was in a great hurry, but how was I going to disturb an angel the height of a five-year-old child, dressed entirely in white, in the middle of who knows what meditations?), and then, while I was wiping my hands on my jeans, trying my hardest not to jump up and down and betray the urgency of the situation – after all, while demons inspire the most extravagant acts, angels incite us to remain dignified – she let go of both doors and approached, in little hops, as if she'd read my mind and possessed enough diabolical blood (we know what kinds of things go on between angels of all species) to make fun of me, and asked me in a clear voice:

"Do you know how to go pee, madame?"

Nostalgia for earthly functions, or do angels have the same needs as us? Instead of launching into an explanation of the question in general, I explained the essence of the installation in a few words so the operation could be carried out in the best way possible, wondering at the same time if the whiter than white of angel apparel gets dirty like the white of mortals. After deciding that it might, I recommended she lift her skirt as high as possible.

Was she thinking that I'd explain it better with a demonstration?

"Thank you," she said, and I thought that perhaps I should offer to help her, but my modesty wouldn't allow it. Can one actually touch angels like that?

Opening one of the doors again, she took a long look at the structure of the hole, and then shook her head.

"Thank you. I think I better go find my mother."

When I returned to Fafner, I saw her in the distance while she was trying to extract another mortal from a car with Belgian plates. Why do they send angels so uninformed of earthly customs, and what missions are they on?

Breakfast: oranges, bread and butter, fig jam, coffee.

A whole morning of "dolce far niente" in the woods.

13:10 Departure. 24°C.

Sun as heavy as lead when we leave the shelter of the woods.

13:26 Roadworks on the highway. We're diverted into the oncoming lanes. Mist produced by the heat. For the first time in 12 or 13 days, we see cars coming towards us.

13:29 Return to the proper side. We advance beneath a white, burning sun.

13:31 Stop: AIRE DU CHIEN BLANC.

Service station, shop, restaurant (not announced on the map): "Relais de l'Auxois".

(Seen from afar, with its peculiar lettering, we read "Relais de l'Amour", which provokes Fafner's jealousy).

Fafner facing: E.S.E.

Lunch: chicken, apples, coffee.

13:55 Departure. 35°C.

13:56 Fortified castle on the left.

14:00 Windmill on the right.

14:01 Close to Autun, Gallic-Roman city.

"Dijon, capital of the duchy of Burgundy".

14:06 Stop: AIRE DU CHAIGNOT.

Beautiful wooded rest area.

Fafner facing: N.

15:30 Time when all cars stop to let their dogs go pee.

16:55 24°C (in the shade).

Dinner: radishes, steak with onions, salad, cheese, coffee.

WHERE WE ATTEMPT TO EXPLAIN,
AS IF THAT WERE POSSIBLE, HAPPINESS

That old obsession that returns once again, leitmotiv of joys and anxieties: the world has no dimensions. In those distant chemistry lessons when they patiently explained that the volume of a gas is determined by its container, why did they never add the essential part of the explanation, that the container couldn't have eternally fixed dimensions either, that nothing prevents attempting the union of infinity by both ends?

Rest stops don't escape the rule. Twice in a row we haven't been able to stifle a brief "oh" of disappointment at the discovery of the ground where we would have to live for several hours or a whole night. A strip of asphalt, in a certain way a twin of the one that continues in a straight line to Lyon or Marseille, with the difference that on this side the vehicles are still and on the other – from which almost nothing separates us – they race along at top speed. A sort of garage entrance, then, except that instead of leading us there, it projects us again, and without any real change of direction or landscape, onto the freeway. But that won't make us renounce the rules of the game. With the same speed as usual we raise the cloth bellows that form our roof, set up our deck chairs on their metal frames, check the horizontal level of the fridge and, as if giving the finger to the ugliness of the rest stop, open up the bed and spread out the sheets, ready for a more intimate revenge. We don't see cars anymore, not even the Super TGV train that passes like a jet plane a very few metres from Fafner. Now there is a chamber whose filtered light grows dimmer as the sky gets cloudy and the thunder begins to rumble. A chamber that transforms into one, into all the clandestine refuges of love. The sky darkens once again, the rain pounds on the roof, but we are

Every once in a while, we have to wash our clothes . . .

. . . and this too is shared.

The results of a valiant effort.

already far away; and the fridge's pilot light, if we manage to see it, could very well be flames in the hearth of a great medieval Scottish bedchamber where we've sought shelter before the coming storm. Fafner opens up as we open ourselves to each other, leaves off being this nice but narrow space where we have to measure our gestures and movements not to bump our funny bones or kick each other or knock over the carton of eggs or the transistor radio. No: he unfurls, immense and vibrant; these partitions are complicit, yielding to our gestures without breaking, and this roof that rises infinitely is an intimate associate when our desires demand more space than Fafner can normally offer. More than once we've ascertained that our embraces do not leave him indifferent. A few years ago we put down to youth and inexperience the only indiscretion we've known him to make: looking to experience things in the same way as us, he let himself get so carried away by passion that his back door opened all at once and we suddenly found ourselves under the stars at the most unexpected moment.

But the dragon has matured since then, and I don't think the doors will open again at the impetus of his delight. This long trip in which nothing prevents us from seeking each other constantly has calmed him, and he's grown in stature. We cannot deny that he gets filled and stretched, overflows with desire, offering us a resistance wherever we want it, protecting us from indiscreet gazes and at the same time making himself very small around us, perhaps the better to feel the slightest tremble of desire. Perhaps, as well, to show us that in these conditions, space is effectively limitless.

Like so many other times, the first glance proved deceptive. What we thought was a stop designed more than anything for demanding bladders or, in the worst case, for drivers to be able to change a tire less riskily than on the freeway, reveals its secrets to us after our siesta, beneath a warm and candid sun.

On the side furthest away from the autoroute (that is, four or five metres from it), Julio discovers a tiny hollow, a little corner of greenery where we can set up the deckchairs, read and drink our aperitif. Although everyone else's freeway seems terribly and even dangerously close, we gradually realize that it's always very far away, that it can't reach us now as we'd feared it might at the beginning of the expedition. Either the madness is getting worse, or we really are gradually entering this limitless space that goes beyond first appearances, designing a second reality that lets us say, exhausted and fatigued and happy, as Julio pours a very cold white burgundy at five in the afternoon, and looking at each other with serenity-filled smiles:

"How wonderful it is here!"

How we are now a limitless space
where reality crystalizes

There are thousands of kilometres between Paris and Toronto, where Diana Cooper-Clark lives, and between Toronto and the Chaignot rest area, where we are now, there are thousands of kilometres multiplied by a mysterious distance immeasurable in kilometres or miles. A distance compounded by the fact that Diana is suddenly included in the trip, closer to us than the inhabitants of the village we can make out ten or fifteen minutes away (this brief walk is unthinkable, and the distance thus absolute, not to mention a total separation of mentalities: Who knows how one of those Burgundian farmers, whose farmhouses look so hospitable, would react if by chance he approached the fence while enjoying the fresh evening breeze and we started to chat: "What a shame we can't visit your village, but, you understand, we're not allowed to leave the autoroute before the 24th of June . . ." Would he back away, shaking his head and saying: "Ah, these Parisians, they're crazier than loons"? Or would he think we were making fun of him? Would he react with unforeseen and possibly grave consequences?).

Diana is part of the trip but she knows nothing about it, and there are suddenly circumstances, which have only been felt as tiny drops of reality barely separated by daily life for the last ten or twelve or eighteen months, crystallizing now, first in an interview she did with Julio that I've just read, in which the interviewer seems just as interested as the interviewee, and in the second place because the entrance of Diana – who, as I've already said, is so far away that she can have no idea of our crazy adventure – into this book, or into what will perhaps be a book, because of an answer she was able to provoke from Julio that has been swirling around in my head for the last

Documentary evidence: typical WC (Aire de Chaignot).

Innocent and apprehensive, the dragon contemplates hands that spring from the earth at the Chaignot rest area.

few minutes as an image of the trip in reverse (or sideways, or just as it is: an impression of a very fine and almost imperceptible thread, to which is added a sensation of total opportunity that is pursuing me). Quoting an Indian metaphysical thinker he doesn't name (does he exist, or is the "quote" nothing more than the perfect illustration of himself?), he says: "When you look at two separate objects, and you begin to look at the gap between the two objects and you concentrate your attention in that gap, in that void between the two objects, then at one moment, you see reality."

I imagine that the two cities, especially when they're reduced for practical purposes to two points on a map, can represent the two objects, and the trajectory between them represents the emptiness between them. For a week and a half now, Paris and Marseille, without needing to look for more or less important circles on the route map, are only two abstract poles that allow us to describe the space between them, and perceive within it (and I return to Diana to thank her for also having spoken of synaesthesia, a word I hadn't actually forgotten but had relegated to the silo of my mind where such useful words pile up), through a slow and patient meditation, a reality that would have been impossible for us to glimpse without this elimination of the departure and the arrival.

The more we advance, the greater liberty we seem to enjoy. And not at all because we are getting close to Marseille. On the contrary, probably the fact of having gained distance from the departure point and at the same time completely lost sight of the end of the journey is what gives it this quality. Little by little we learn not just to look at the space the hypothetical Indian philosopher spoke of, but to *be it* with all that we are. And this space between objects, from the moment our gaze leaves them outside, from one side to the other of the field of vision, is it not by definition limitless?

At this very moment, Julio raises his head, listens, and warns Fafner: "*Attenti!*" That noise he heard, was it the grunting of a rhinoceros or perhaps more likely a hippopotamus?

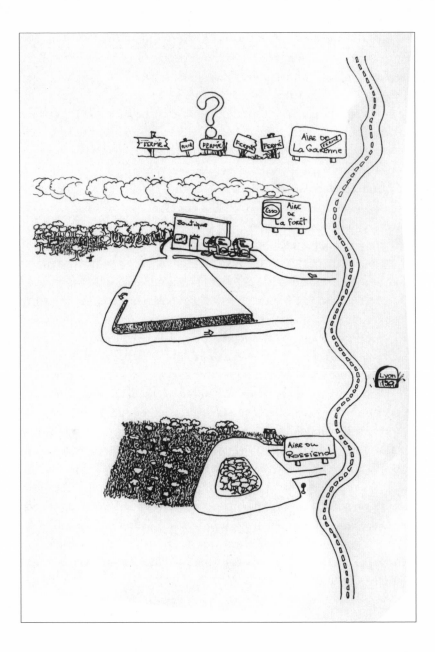

OSITA ALONE IN THE WOODS (SUITE)

At the entrance to the real woods there is an invisible dog tied to a tree by a red leash that someone has taken the precaution of fastening with a double knot. I wouldn't understand its true function until I'd followed the path that advances through the woods, far, so far that I was suddenly frightened. Shadows surrounded me, and the path went on into infinity beneath immense trees. Behind me, nothing: more trees, as if even retracing my steps I could only sink deeper into the gloom. However, I perfectly remember the landscape seen from this side at the moment we came off the freeway: a sparse little wood, like we often find at the edges of the rest stops. A little wood that ended, after twenty metres or so, at a field. And nevertheless I keep advancing without perceiving the edge of this old, dense leafy glade, whose shade is only cut here and there by spots of sun that filter through the dense foliage. I don't hear the distant noise of the cars that has accompanied us now for so long. My own footsteps barely let me hear a faint sliding through the undergrowth.

The forbidden. I know no fence has blocked my way, and nevertheless . . . Will the demons take perversity to the point of stationing an *invisible* Cerberus at the entrance to forbidden landscapes?

With the pretext (for whom? Am I talking to a double who judges?) of getting a little exercise, I run back: get out of this threatening shade. I only stop when I see good old Fafner placidly settled beside Julio while he hammers furiously away at his typewriter. Nothing has changed. Perhaps the light, a little lower. Danger, however, was close. It was real and terrifying.

(Other possible explanation: the owners of the rhinoceros underestimated his strength, and he ate them before taking flight. Serves them right

Overcome by gluttony, la Osita savours two ice cream cones (raspberry and pistachio).

if they think they can tame a rhinoceros with a red leather leash fit for a Parisian Pekinese. But I suspect that the rhinoceros, in spite of his ferocious air, is inclined to be vegetarian.)

8:00   18°C. Cloudy.

   Breakfast: oranges, almond cakes, coffee.

11:25   Departure. Sunny, 24°C.

11:27   On our left, a village and 12th century castle.

11:28   On our right, the Burgundy Canal, which we valiantly cross.

11:29   A barge advances along the canal at the same pace as us. We think of the *Bevinco*, Jean Thiercelins's boat.

11:30   We cross the canal for the second time.

   Viaduct of Pont d'Ouche.

11:32   A closed rest stop.

11:34   Really, they've closed the rest stop on us (renovation and expansion). Sabotage?

   A very steep hill.

   Bligny-sur-Ouche State-Owned Forest.

11:40   Stop: AIRE DE LA FORET.

   Three star boutique.

   Fafner facing: S.S.E.

12:45 (approximately):   Vision in the WC (see text).

   Lunch: pâté sandwiches, cold meat (steak), onions, tomatoes, compote, coffee.

13:15   30°C.

20:48   One might say that all the demons of hell have been unleashed against Fafner. We resist while the storm rages in the night. Hail, lightning, thunder, torrential rain, nothing left out.

   Dinner: veal cutlets with lemon, flageolets, ice cream, coffee.

A facial expression betraying an important scientific discovery.

OF THE TITANIC STRUGGLE THAT THE
EXPLORERS UNLEASHED AGAINST AN ENEMY
WHOSE WEAPONS ARE SILENCE AND PINCERS

We would never presume that this expedition, no matter how many risks and vicissitudes might arise, could be comparable to the one Werner Herzog imagined (or put into images) in *Aguirre, The Wrath of God*. Here there are no Indians or arrows dipped in curare, much less monkeys; to tell the whole truth, there aren't even any Spaniards like in the film, because on this voyage all we've been finding in any quantities so far are English people, followed closely by Germans and Belgians, all this apart from the natives who somehow give the impression of being washed away by this international deluge.

If we think by analogy that the French are the Indians of this highway, we have to admit they proceed with enormous discretion and tend to relieve themselves as quickly as possible, eat a sandwich, and return to their Renault or Talbot canoes as though what happens outside terrifies them considerably. *Madre mía*, have they always traveled like this? How did Jacques Cartier manage, oh gods above? And Bougainville? These natives we meet in the rest areas don't even seem like they could discover a café in the Latin Quarter; it's true that they would also be frightened there by the clientele of varied foreigners who plant their flags in said places of recreation. For all these reasons and by way of synthesis, we may conclude that our slow advance from north to south is being carried out without wicked ambushes, deadly traps, untimely appearances of leopards, serpents, or any other of the many calamities that drove Lope de Aguirre to kill everybody, including his daughter, before disappearing into the Orinoco covered in mosquitoes and monkeys. Granted, but the time has come to talk about ants.

La Osita buys horrid knickknacks, but she has such fun with them!

Fafner at coffee time.

As everyone knows, the ant is a charming little creature when found meandering over a table or trying to scale our aunt's ankle. Only a despicable person would take pleasure in tormenting an ant, who will only bite if we try to squeeze its head between our fingers. There is no one I appreciate more than an ant, paradigmatically laborious insect, Maeterlinck, Fabre, etc. The only problem is that, like Nazis and rock fans, ants never come alone but rather in overwhelming multitudes, and the charm of the individual dissolves into the horror of the brutish mass, exactly as happened to us last night when, as we were getting ready to rest in Fafner's warm and welcoming belly, we discovered that the industrious insects in question had climbed up the tires in order to invade in their thick legions every invadable nook and cranny of the dragon, who has such places in abundance, and that while seven hundred and forty of them tried to finish off a stick of butter, several thousand proliferated beside the salami, the salted crackers and the six bananas bought that very day with the intention of making a hearty rice *à la cubana*.

I don't know if Carol let out the half-anguished, half-outraged cry that is standard in these cases, and whether I seconded it with one of those curses I've been famous for since way back when; I do know that we instantly perceived the danger, that we launched into a choreographed number next to which Fred Astaire's best sequence would have seemed like inane stamping, and that in a few minutes we'd beat the hell out of the majority of the evil attackers. Justly proud of such a crushing (never so true) counteroffensive, we decide to reward ourselves with a nightcap, duly bottled in Scotland, before we embark towards that Cithaeron where, contrary to the opinion of eminent Hellenists, Aphrodite and Morpheus alternate their golden rhythms all night long.*

I hardly need add that as soon as we'd slipped into bed, we began to feel in regions rather prone to itching the pincers of five or six ants who were

*It's true: the classic dyads are Aphrodite/Ares and Hypnos/ Thanatos, never Aphrodite/ Hypnos, except in Fafner, maybe because he's closer to Valhalla than to Olympus.

Where it can be observed that the consumer society wastes no time on the freeway.

indignant to find we were dislodging them from the white steppe where they were wandering in full Siberian autosuggestion. Killing them was easy, since they were black on white, but what we didn't know about was the latent presence of legions of reserves, crouching in barely visible corners of the dragon. So that was how Carol, who around three in the morning began one of those extravagant bouts of insomnia that later keep her sleeping straight through to nine-thirty, discovered that along the plastic edging that bordered the little window beside the bed, the ants had initiated a procession that was perhaps religious but no less unsettling insofar as they were marching towards the foot of the bed, in other words to the part of the bed where we had our feet. Sweet and discreet as ever, Carol did not wake me; her sense of sacrifice combined with her insomnia made her spend two hours with one finger in the air, letting it fall gently upon each new ant that crossed the ledge, until the procession lost its mystic drive or she fell asleep. In the morning we still found a few individuals who, their military spirit now completely annihilated, devoted themselves to tracing erratic hieroglyphics on the floor, ceiling or pillows.

The struggle had been cruel, but today, almost a week later, we can guarantee that there are only seven or eight ants still crouching in Fafner. As you can see, the freeway is no bed of roses; had we not reacted in time, the police who circulate in the rest areas might perhaps have had the horrendous surprise of finding our skeletons, not to mention the butter, entirely devoured. We triumphed because we knew these terrible insects' tactics, which consist in sowing panic in the enemy by way of speed en masse. That UNESCO translator put it very well who, having to put the following sentence into Spanish: "*Comme disait feu le Président Roosevelt, rien n'est à craindre hormis la crainte elle-même* [As the late President Roosevelt said, we've nothing to fear but fear itself]", produced the memorable version to which we might just owe our lives: "*Como decía con ardor el presidente Roosevelt, el miedo a las hormigas lo crean ellas mismas* [As President Roosevelt so ardently said, the fear of ants is created by ants themselves]".

A *CLOSED REST AREA,*

ANOTHER WHERE THEY SELL BUDDHAS,

AND EROS PROPOSES HIS CEREMONIES.

On Friday, just before midday, we sadly left the Chaignot rest area, a beautiful wooded stop where we would have liked to spend a day or two working, reading, listening to music, letting that time beyond the reach of clocks that gives us such great peace flow. We especially regretted it since the map of the autoroute promised us a particularly unenjoyable day: a first stop that didn't even enter the green of a Burgundy woodland and a second that promised a service station. We knew from experience that the first would be nothing but a strip parallel to the freeway, with no protection against the noise or the sun (which, as we advanced towards the south, grew hotter and hotter), and would offer us no possibility to set ourselves up as comfortably as we'd become accustomed to doing. The second, for its part, promised to be nothing more than a puddle of asphalt whose monotony would be broken only by gasoline tanks and the shade of heavy cargo vehicles parked around them, a stop where we would sleep in almost the same conditions as in a supermarket parking lot.

But long before embarking on the journey we'd decided we would not cheat, at least not very often, and we told ourselves that if the experience was not agreeable, it might be amusing. After all, after so many rest areas in which, to put it plainly, we'd had a great time, readers might be asking themselves why, if we wanted to spend a month camping, it was necessary to put on such an act. Perhaps it might well have been time our two intrepid explorers had to confront the worries that befit such a dangerous voyage.

Neither of us would have taken this attitude of mind as far as masochism, and when at 11:32 we caught sight of a P covered with a sort of tarp, we felt something like a tickling in the stomach. Perhaps that didn't mean anything, for in fact we hadn't seen the P, but instinctively we recognized the shape and dimensions of the sign announcing a rest area. Would we have to spend all day and all night in proximity to a horrible service station? (That had already happened to us when we experienced the first sabotage, on the second day of the expedition; but it was still young then and we knew many beautiful rest areas were awaiting us further on, while now, after two weeks on the freeway, we had the certainty that each day we were approaching a region where most of them are bad, at least as far as we remembered.)

11:34 am on Friday the 4th of June. We are passing the rest area, which is indeed closed, although occupied by an army of men dressed in yellow-orange working among mountains of gravel and sand. The next time we pass this way it'll be a great rest area where it will be a pleasure to stop; but for the moment it has ceased to exist, like a movie star when it's time for their facelift or annual silicone injection. The next stop – the one with the gasoline tanks – will have to count for two.

11:40: It's not easy to suppress a slight shudder when we catch sight of the huge P/1000 m. gradually approaching the windshield. The autoroute, which we don't feel we travel very frequently, has at this level at least the advantage of offering a splendid view over beautiful landscapes. We drive at 30 or 40 kilometres per hour after having passed the closed rest stop, as if to make the lush greenness that spreads on either side of the freeway as far as the eye can see last, trying to prolong that not being anywhere which suddenly seems so pleasant. But Fafner advances inevitably, as soon as you press his accelerator and no matter how gently you do so, towards what's in front of him, and not towards either side with that scenery we'd never seen so well during any of our previous journeys. Despite our love for this region, we knew then that its immediate role was to allow itself to be crossed as quickly as possible. That's how it is; when you're really going towards the lavender and thyme you forget you can also appreciate the sweet

*Put this in your car and you'll have
no excuse not to be happy.*

*What more could you ask of
the modern world?*

undulations of Burgundy with its countless greens, alfalfa fields, cows who seem to be expecting some nineteenth-century landscape painter.

Fafner advances, then, in spite of our silent prayers, posed to gods who obviously don't travel on the freeway, to make this acceleration go in reverse. P/2oom. We're here. And we give thanks to whoever closed the first rest area and forced us to accept this little cheat. (Where does this sensation come from that if we hadn't been so happy to escape the first rest stop, which no matter how you look at it corresponds to our negative suspicion, this would have been more honest?) To our surprise, the rest area is one of the loveliest we've seen so far. Virtually private paths enter a big forest, and Fafner heads down them with his unerring instinct. It's true, at the entrance to the parking lot there is a super-service station, a shop where you can buy anything, for example a metre-high porcelain Buddha, or a gigantic teddy bear for the modest sum of 850 francs, and also coffee, and hot or cold sandwiches. But behind it is the woodland with its secret, shady paths, and an ideal place to set up the dragon.

That could have been all, the meals relished beneath the trees, the long siesta with the gently caressing breeze barely stirring the curtains, the delicious baguette found miraculously in the shop, and it would already have been a lot to ask from a single day. Only fate brought us to the true secret of the surprise, which will perhaps be the subject of another text when its effect has ripened in some corner of my spirit.

The moment arrived when we had to decide whether to wash the dishes beside Fafner, making use of Jean's jerry can, or at the sanitary facilities we could see in the distance. We didn't know if there would be an exterior sink there that would make rinsing the cups and glasses easier.

"I'll go look, and then we'll decide."

"No, let me go," said Julio.

"I'll do it, because I have to go anyway."

I take the path that leads through a little woods towards the ultramodern WC we can barely make out from the place where we've set ourselves up. From twenty metres away I observe that the doors on both sides are open,

La Forêt rest area: the sanitary facilities where the vision appeared.

Scientific detail of our set-up at the Rossignol rest area.

but after another five steps I freeze. Not only because in the wide-open door of the ladies' side I see a pair of buttocks, and especially the shadow that divides them since the daylight that pours in concentrates there; and not even because after having realized that it is indeed a naked bottom, I discover that it's beautiful and white and firm, and that in the space of the door is a perfectly sketched body of a svelte, graceful woman leaning slightly forward with a gesture stolen from some symbolist painting; no, what causes the second and true surprise of the day is realizing, with a mixture of admiration and inexplicable nostalgia, that the most intriguing things are the black stockings that envelop the long legs that seem suspended on top of high heels, and the garters, just as black, that uphold them.

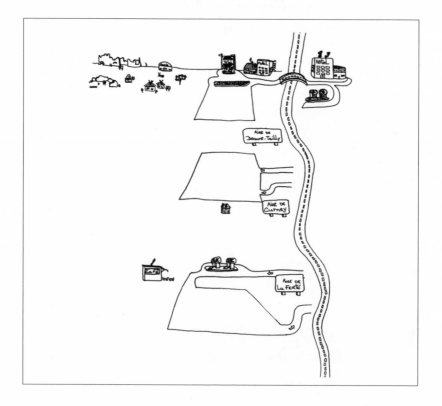

8am 20°C.

> Breakfast: oranges, almond cake, coffee.

9:06 Departure.

9:11 Bessey-en-Chaume Pass. Altitude: 565 metres.

9:16 Stop: AIRE DU ROSSIGNOL.

Panoramic views.

Fafner facing: N.N.E.

12:30 36°C.

12:32 Departure.

12:33 Pass Beaune.

12:43 Stop: AIRE DE BEAUNE-TAILLY.

Fafner facing: S.S.E.

> Lunch (in the rest area's "bistrot"): soup (only Julio), hors d'oeuvre trolley (Carol), beef bourguignon, local cheeses.

17:00 57°C (in the sun), which has not prevented us from exploring, like the intrepid expeditionaries we are, the "Archéodrome".

The rest area is the most gigantic one we've seen up till now. We spend the night in the hotel.

> Dinner: we forgot to write down what we ate.

WHERE THE EXPLORERS DELVE INTO THE PAST
AND MEET – DANTES DE NOS JOURS – JULIUS CAESAR,
EUGENE SUE AND VERCINGETORIX

Every expedition assumes that in some way Marco Polo, Columbus or Shackleton had not lost touch with their inner child. Mine, in any case, is entirely bright-eyed and bushy-tailed as each rest area opens its peacock's tail (sometimes a little sparsely feathered, sometimes splendid and irides-cent) to fill him with wonder, caterpillars, ants and trucks with charming slogans, like for example the one for SPEEDY SOUP that just went by as I was finishing this sentence.

Today it's the Beaune–Tailly rest area (+ motel, oh bliss!), where the sign with its underlined name like on them all also includes a strange word that slips stealthily into the caverns of the imaginary: ARCHÉODROME. But since the boy is the father of the man, we begin by checking into the motel, where a passably brothelesque room wraps us in mauve shadows, mistaken lights, a bathtub inviting us to feel like dolphins in perfumed foam, and the siesta that follows all of that, the siesta of love, the deepest of siestas where bodies rest like Siamese twins, arms and thighs and hands overlapping, interweaving in the final loss of all identity, nirvana of blurred pillows, whirlwinded sheets.

When we get to the Archéodrome, the disturbing silhouette of which stands out like a total fracture in this uniform time of gas pumps, general stores and parking lots, the first impression of entering a museum makes us smile; the historic anachronism seems almost a hoax in this unsurprising till now continuum, since after paying for our tickets we begin a trajectory starting from the Burgundian neolithic and culminating in the national epic of the

In the Beaune-Tailly motel, la Osita plays with el Lobo and the mirror.

At the Archéodrome museum (Beaune-Tailly), this image from the past tends to close its eyes to the freeway.

siege of Alesia and the decisive confrontation between Vercingetorix and Julius Caesar, here looking more like Asterix versus Marcello Mastroiani.

But the child keeps watch, begins to tour with growing wonder the reconstructions of huts, tombs, farming methods, arriving finally at the tall defences of the Roman camp between the besieged city and the rearguard of the invading force menaced by the coalition of the Gallic tribes that heed Vercingetorix's call. A video then shows us the phases of the battle, in which the military genius of Julius Caesar triumphs over disorderly enemies superior in number. (Against his will but obliged by a crushing logic, the voiceover admits step-by-step the reasons the Roman eagles would crush the pre-French.)

That's when I start to live in another way all that I've seen and heard this afternoon, when the child emerges from almost sixty years of slumber and once again understands in his way the episodes he's being shown and told. The book was a Spanish translation of *The Mysteries of the People* by Eugène Sue: two large-format, double-column volumes that had me immersed for a month in a fabulous history of France from the Druids up to, I think, Napoleon III, by way of the Merovingian monarchs, Joan of Arc, the religious wars, the revolution and empire. Of all that, which I could also have remembered in other museums (so many times I've relived fragments out of simple association of ideas), the Roman conquest of the Gauls overcomes me today *in situ*, with the double force of memory and its evocation in the very terrain of its terrible epilogue. I don't think the battle of Alesia appeared in Eugène Sue's novel, but the awakening of the Gauls against the foreign invader certainly did, as did Vercingetorix's desperate act to try to impose the reason of liberty against the Roman machine advancing league by league, as one advances page by page in Caesar's Commentaries on the Gallic Wars.

As for Caesar, who as a boy I held in the esteem every well-lived boyhood dedicates to warriors and emperors of antiquity, Eugène Sue's portrait of him scandalized and offended me. The hero of Pharsalus, lover of Cleopatra, is seen as a cruel and career-minded officer, lacking in imagination and generosity, a cold, chess-playing tactician with his legionaries, incapable of measuring the greatness of his enemy (which is true, since he took Vercingetorix to Rome and had him decapitated on the day of his triumph). I remember it took many hours of reading, and Sue's talent, to persuade me to accept this version of Caesar, but the moment arrived when the boy went over definitively to the Gauls and lived a war at their sides that the history books and Caesar himself had always showed from his.

And just a moment ago, looking at the reconstruction of the traps the Romans set for their enemies in Alesia, and which remind one of those the Vietnamese used against the Yankee invaders, the most terrible and anguished moment of my reading invaded me with all its power: the episode in which nature lays in her turn the most horrific trap for the Roman soldiers. I experienced it again as if I were reading the novel in my house in Banfield, in that moment of childhood when everything was sight, smell, sound and touch, I again saw that legionary who advances like a heavy, slow coleopteran inside his armour and begins to sink in a quaking bog, what the novel calls quicksand, and in which he is submerged bit by bit, struggling desperately to find a handhold, disappearing until only his head with its helmet remain, and then the quicksand closes over him and only a few bubbles of asphyxiation break the surface, to the final horror of the boy possessed by that nightmare vision.

While we were returning to the motel I wondered ironically what I would find if I reread Sue's novel, and that passage in particular (along with the death of Joan of Arc, and the adventures of *Fergán el Cantero* and *Josefino del Francotopo*, and who knows what they were called in the original). But I wondered without risk of doing so, because if there's one thing I know it's that I'm not going to reread certain childhood books, or those from other times, like *Les Enfants Terribles* or *La Condition Humaine*. This Archéodrome is pleasant and accessible; the other ones, the deep down ones, will remain in me just as they were once and forever known; they will stay in the transparent sepulchre of memory, like the terracotta army that guarded the rest of the founding prince of China for so many centuries.

The Archéodrome at l'Aire de Beaune-Tailly, where Vercingetorix and Julius Caesar fought their final match.

BEGINNING AND END OF THE WORLD
FROM A SCHUBERT QUARTET

Looking at the road map, I can see once again that we're heading in the right direction. Indeed, those who are returning to Paris and want to stop level with La Forêt rest area have to settle for Le Creux Moreau; the fact that they're both marked on the map with a little sign showing a brand of gasoline and a man perched precariously on top of a tire (incidentally, some aspects of these symbols should perhaps be revised: can disabled people recognize themselves in this new type of unicyclist?) changes nothing in the magic of the names. And at the next stop, there where we rest in the

Other people's autoroute.

Rossignol rest area, the travellers who take a break on their way back to the capital will find themselves in the Bois de . . . Corbeaux.

Prudent as ever, we explore the possibilities of our new stop thoroughly before choosing a definitive site. It's extremely important, given that at ten in the morning the sun makes you feel like you're in the middle of the Sahara, and the possibilities of the nightingale rest area aren't so many (it's clear that having opted for the designation "panorama", which it fully deserves, they've taken the precaution of not obstructing the view with trees or any supplementary installations). There is a tiny island of pines between two tracks for vehicles, which together form a rhomboid, and a little further on, a field we could drive across stretches down to shelter beneath the only tree at the bottom; but the rains of the previous night have been violent, and we worry Fafner might get stuck. Therefore we set our dragon up very close to the little island, at a prudent distance from the WCs, and we take immediate possession of a table under the trees (although it's still early, travellers are already starting to stop with evident gastronomical intentions, and since the heat tends to excite and exasperate drivers as well as passengers, the results are foreseeable). In a few seconds, thanks to the experience acquired over the course of the expedition, we raise the roof, get the fridge level, set up our deckchairs on the shadiest side of the table, and the table in question becomes unmistakably occupied by the business of typewriters, books, bottles, glasses, cameras and a soda siphon (to dazzle the incredulous).

We then settle down to have a nice drink, in the first place to congratulate ourselves for having been smart enough to arrive in time to occupy the best place (this could seem egotistical, friend and reader, but just think that where the ordinary traveller makes one stop in a six or eight hour trip, we are pausing in the course of a thirty-three day journey), and in the second place because we're happy, and some remnant or effluence of the long, beautiful night we've just experienced causes us to act as if the fiesta is still ongoing – and it's also true that this trip is an unending fiesta of life – not to mention that all this helps us to start other activities, given that we haven't

In an impressive exhibition of the tools of the trade, witness the birth of the page you're now reading.

set up our typewriters here only to keep some guy from Lyon from coming to eat his sausages beside us, but also because we want to work and it's well known that a little drink for inspiration never does any harm.

The important thing after all is that we're quite a distance from the freeway, given that the Rossignol rest area is a sort of mound that overlooks it. At the same time, I have the impression that up till now I've never had such a clear concept of the autoroute; I've never seen it stretching off so far in both directions, never had such an impression of harmony by following all the curves and slopes that I can, thanks to the location of the rest area, take in with a single glance. Given the elevation of the terrain, the trucks and cars pass in silence, no roar, no clanging gears, although the Paris–to–Lyon route descends, and the Lyon–to–Paris side climbs considerably. Speed itself seems abolished by this hush; only the slow, harmonious, infinite movement of anonymous yet perfectly discernible shapes can be seen, and seems to correspond to some unfathomable, just and profound need.

I set up my typewriter and realize I've forgotten something inside Fafner. On my way back, I feel trapped by the view of the other side, a landscape that the morning mists had hidden from us when we arrived. Trapped, and nevertheless I spin around and realize that it's the same everywhere. I take off from the rest area, more winged than a Chagall character; I am that distant mountain, I drink the blue of those trees that I can barely make out as distinctive entities, I slip down the quarry way over there, and always in the rest area and always still, the spin continues to the point of vertigo, that vertigo one gets in rare moments of life with 360 degree vision that annihilates and creates at the same time.

A brief musical phrase begins to make its way through the whirlwind, similar to the nightingale who tests out his scale as night is falling, before launching into his song wholeheartedly. Two, three notes, whose gravity seem to arise from the grandeur of the landscape. A beat, another, and it's that Schubert quartet which resembles no other, and forgetting what I'd come to look for, I climb inside Fafner where I know we have a recording of this very quartet, and on which I throw myself frequently with that kind

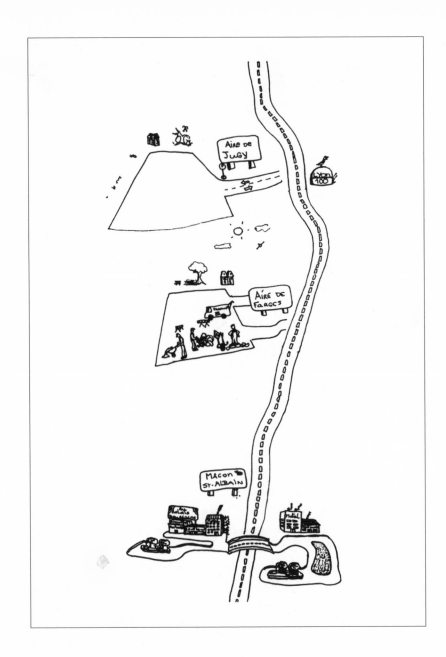

of inevitable violence in moments I cannot define or even relate to each other, and so in less time than it takes me to say so, I'm sitting in the back seat, joined to the tape player by the headphone cord like an extraterrestrial creature. The first notes begin, mournful and grave, as the world must once have begun, a music-pain like the landscape that surrounds me, of which I'm part, violin and cello; the grave notes interrupt like a wound and the unexpected sharp heals, and then comes the slow, so slow and marvelous fusion of everything, the harmony searching itself out, hoarding the surrounding mountains and even the tourists who've started arriving. In the middle of the rest area, the doors open, enclosed in silence; in an exterior silence the world is born and I see them, I see them all, not just el Lobo who hasn't stopped typing there beneath the trees, but also the couple who get out of a 4L right beside Fafner and who look, with an inquisitive smile on their lips, at the cassette player, the headphones, my face and my hands that, yes, direct it all, again, as they once directed the formation of the landscape, form the mist that rises faster and faster all around. I see them, I do. But not from my body, not with these eyes which have barely smiled at them. No, I see them from where I listen and which cannot be spoken, from the heart of the stringed instruments, from within the brain of a long dead musician and yet still there, floating and submerging way up above the mountain, with no wall or window or city or house around him, I touch the heart, birth and expansion of the music like the view: in each musician's finger guiding the arcs like so many other lovers, each foot maintaining the delicate balance of the instrument, each chin resting on its pillow without leaving a trace: with each note, those things that don't exist and that nevertheless, in moments like this, are all of creation and the finality of the world, I am there, as big as all these mountains, I am the deep quarries, I am the time the cassette lasts, at the same time the movement and stillness that is one, and not even the Germans who approach the car to see whether I'm *recording* something, nor the family that stops, shocked, to stare with incredulous eyes, can break that perfect circle. Only, perhaps, that little boy who came and sat on the running board and who, turning his back on me, began to sway bit by bit to the rhythm of the quartet, entered consciously, really sharing the experience, even if they're all part of it.

Rossignol, panoramic parking lot, do your birds sing now, for those who know how to hear, that beautiful Schubert theme that transformed a rest area into the beginning and end of the world?

WHERE THE READER SHALL AGREE
THAT A ROSE IS A ROSE IS A ROSE

How many times, under the effect of surprise, does one lose the true surprise enclosed therein? That's perhaps what happened to us today on our way to the reception of the Beaune rest area motel, where someone we'll probably never see has cultivated perfectly shaped and dazzlingly coloured roses. How to *describe* a colour that spreads over the petals as if it were the most natural thing in the world, and which is at the same time texture, consistency, light and shadow, warmth that does not keep a sort of certainty of coolness from dominating the whole? Futile to explain that the most startling were a colour we'd have to place between red and pink, carefully rationing the delicate droplets of orange that enhance its luminosity; for even if a reader by rapturous chance managed to conceive a mental vision of this hue, they would still lack the singularly heavy and transparent velvet that seemed to convey the defiance calmly growing there, a hundred or so metres from the freeway, its noise, rhythms and combustion gases. We could do nothing but stand there, quench the thirst for that colour, that texture, surprised at finding that such emotion can still be born of a flower, and feeling a little silly at having no other possible reaction than saying *oh*, how lovely. And walking off to the motel room, key in hand.

But who's to say that this colour, which is a surprise in itself, doesn't exist only to lure the spectator away, by way of the surprise itself, from something else, from a key hidden inside the petals, an even greater beauty protected by a lesser rung of the same phenomenon? That last look, should it not have whetted our appetite even more, rather than sating it? Or must we accept that genre of beauty just as it's presented, as if nothing could surpass it?

We'll never know if that perfect flower hid a second, even more marvelous. And not being botanists, it would have been impossible to go and see, without destroying what we'd been offered as a free and unexpected pleasure.

Breakfast: orange juice, bread and butter, croissants, apricot jam, red currant jelly, coffee (in the motel).

10:30 35°C.

10:45 We leave behind us the comforts of the motel.

11:05 Departure.

11:07 Département de Saône-et-Loire.

11:15 Stop: AIRE DE LA CURNEY.

Fafner facing: E.S.E.

Lunch: corned beef, tomatoes, onions, Morvan cheese, coffee.

19:19 40°C. Departure.

19:32 Stop: AIRE DE LA FERTÉ.

Fafner facing: S.S.W.

Dinner: sweet and sour pork, cheese, coffee.

W*HERE IT SHALL BE SEEN THAT OUR*
PROTAGONISTS ARE NOT DISCOURAGED BY THE MOST
IGNOBLE PERSECUTIONS, AND THEIR UNSHAKEABLE
DETERMINATION TO SUCCEED IN THEIR MISSION
IS PROVEN ONCE MORE

Good or bad rest areas, everything was going swimmingly, and we were getting ever more used to the anonymity and total freedom the freeway kindly granted us. It was enough to bestow a smile upon the gendarmes who approached every once in a while to look us over, especially when Fafner was hidden deep in the woods, to feel safe;* the defenders of law and order were never the same ones, and up until then we hadn't witnessed two police patrols in a single rest area. But here, a little before Mâcon, when we had the impression of having achieved a cruising speed thanks to which the freeway transformed into a kind of hidden land, inaccessible to any rhythm other than our own, it is here that *they* begin to grow impatient and show themselves, at first timidly, but eventually unveiling a strategy that, subtle though it may be, remains clear, at least to our eyes.

This feeling of freedom, has it led us to let down our defences, or was the attack prepared several rest areas back? Everything began shortly after we crossed the Burgundy Canal twice. We might well have wondered whether those two serpents that are the freeway and canal really do cross each other twice within such a short distance . . . Had we not been diverted in the direction of a false set, subterfuge worthy of a Charlie Chaplin film, separating us

*As to why we might not have felt safe, see pp. 15–17.

184

from the real autoroute the better to trap us in a net spread unscrupulously across our route? We know the enemy well enough to realize that any undertaking based on the imagination seems subversive to them, and to induce failure they'll do everything in their power, which is, alas, immense, so it just remains to us to thank our gods and goddesses that we are but tiny prey in their eyes, otherwise our journey would have been reduced to Paris–Corbeil or, with luck, Paris–Fontainebleau.

The way things are going, it's thanks to *them* that we're now installed in the Crêches rest area, working like crazy, in spite of the resignation this parking lot and the reigning temperature might have been expected to induce, urging us more towards a siesta than towards our typewriters. But we type furiously, with the precise intention of convincing them we are writing a book about the autoroute. We could meditate extensively on the irony and benefits of persecution, but let's go back to the Burgundy Canal

The first and unsettling sign that we are being watched.

The threats are more concrete at the Crêches rest area, where the espionage becomes unbearable.

Under the pretext of various jobs, the siege closes in and we must flee.

and our first premonitions (see p. 23, where we told of the beginnings of the adventure; in light of what happened later, maybe we'd have to consider what role the vision in the WC of the La Forêt rest area played. Mightn't she, Mata Hari of parking lots, have had the mission of luring Julio into an ambush? And what if it had been him who'd gone to wash the dishes?).

Despite the closure of one rest area – the reader knows by now that we don't get discouraged by such a minor detail – we cheerfully followed our course, and spent a day and a marvelous night at La Forêt, which had surprises and delights already described in store for us. But as I write this sentence I feel a strange sensation behind me. When I turn around I notice – the opposite would be impossible given that discretion is not one of the strong points of secondary cronies of the "company" – two well-built individuals, one six metres behind me, the other twenty-five or thirty and leaning against a truck that could quite easily be transformed into a special patrol wagon and on which can be read *Laboratoires de Saône-et-Loire*, watching us without moving and as if they're only waiting for a sign to pounce. Remaining totally calm, I remove the lens cap from my trusty Canon, which is always within reach, and turn back towards the two subjects. The one who was behind me disappears in the direction of the WCs as if at that very moment he'd been overcome by a sudden colic, while the one by the truck crouches down to check the state of the right rear tire for the umpteenth time.

Perhaps they thought (they must have felt very disappointed if one of their spies told them just how thrilled we were to have to change our plans because of the closed rest area) that our good old dragon would run out of breath before he'd be able to clear the Bessey-en-Chaume hill, especially after the excitement that had agitated us during the previous night's storm (had it really been hail or had *they* taken advantage of the nasty weather to install agitators in the trees? Does anyone remember having seen, felt or heard hailstones the size of golf balls falling between 22:48 and 23:03 on the 4th of June?), but Fafner gathers all his courage in his four wheels and, inspired by our patience, triumphs over all obstacles, whether it's the incredible quantity of trucks on the freeway or the road works that force him to perform slaloms worthy of an Olympic champion.

If up till now our good humour and the unreasonableness of our objective had been able to annoy the enemy, the long hours we spent in the hotel at the Beaune-Tailly rest area must have driven them finally over the edge, convinced as they were that everything should remain within very specific and generally quite restrictive limits. Did they think the sight of a thick cable that started from the entrance door was going to impress us? We might have wondered if it could have been an alarm system or a crudely installed microphone, directing a friendly rude gesture towards it just in case that were the situation. Did they think such an obvious sight of an electronic system was going to cure us of our appetite for adventure, or diminish the attractions of the bed, the bathtub or the restaurant where we ate an excellent dinner well accompanied by a regional wine? It could well be, on the other hand, that they'd decided to give us a little break, with the hope that we'd let our guard down again, thinking that in the end there were no reasons to think they were really interested in our expedition, which would lead us to give the game away. (Another hypothesis: they were getting fed up with sleeping in the freeway garbage cans, and the fact that they were apparently provided with no other refuge could explain the proliferation of these receptacles in the rest areas . . . unless they advanced from one to the next, a modern version of a Shakespearean forest.)

Be that as it may, on Sunday at 11:05, still a little dizzy from pleasure, we left the Beaune rest area, more decided than ever to see the expedition through to its end.

There's nothing to note about Le Curney rest area, except perhaps the decrease in the number of English cars and corresponding increase of Belgians. Also, the heavy trucks seem to multiply at a rather suspicious rate, not to mention the lettering they flaunt, and if they do speak (one swallow does not make a summer) of the imaginative powers of bureaucrats in the respective companies, they also arouse doubts over their faculties of concealment: who is really going to believe that trucks with names in enormous letters like SPEEDY SOUP, FRANCE MACARON, HERMETIC UNITY or PHILOSOPHER, not to mention a whole fleet of GAY persued at a hundred and twenty kilometres per hour by an enormous TRANSMEC, can be transporting merchandise essential to daily life from one city to another?

All this does not impede us from carrying on normally with our activities. After finding an entirely agreeable corner of the rest area that's not by a long shot among the most interesting we've seen so far, we get down to work, reading and chatting calmly. We see a truck from the highways authority go by, and then another; we don't pay them too much attention, accustomed as we are to seeing these employees arrive dressed in orange overalls to clean the WCs and the sinks, empty the garbage cans and restock the toilet paper.

At 19:23, an obvious attempt to throw us off track: suddenly, on this autoroute, which we know full well is called "du soleil", a sign is erected saying in big letters:

AUTOROUTE LOUHANS
LONS-LE-SAUNIER

But nothing convinces us of such a thing, much less when in the distance we can already make out the buildings of Chalon.

At 19:32 we arrive at La Ferté rest area, whose most obvious advantage is without doubt the excellent breakfast offered at a reasonable price in the restaurant. Barely have we raised the roof bellows when we find ourselves surrounded by cars with trailers. Once again, a profusion of English license plates. (The reader, whose knowledge of the autoroute is necessarily limited, will perhaps not understand why that detail – surrounded by trailers after all – holds our attention. Just a glance around La Ferté rest area would suffice to realize that a real traveller would do nothing but drive in and straight out of the rest area, instead of setting up among heavy trucks and garbage cans.) All night long we hear the sounds of mysterious arrivals, while it seemed that all the men in the rest area had chosen to use Fafner's parking place as a urinal, so that every fifteen or twenty minutes we felt ourselves transported to a mysterious Villa d'Este of the autoroute.

At five, already up, we have the clear impression of something closing round us. Just past seven we make our getaway.

Breakfast: orange juice, croissants, *pain au chocolat*, coffee.

7:18 Departure.

7:21 On the right, a 12th-century chapel.

7:26 Stop: AIRE DE JUGY.

Horrible.

Fafner facing: E.

7:40 Departure after having duly explored the rest area.

7:46 Stop: AIRE DU FARGES.

Just as horrible.

We colonize the only table where there is a little (very little) shade.

Concerto for jackhammer and unidentified instruments.

Two Argentines — or Uruguayans — sit down with a thermos to drink maté. Given the situation back home, we prefer to avoid all contact.

Lunch: Breton pâté, chickpea and onion salad.

18:16 Gendarmes cars patrol, workers who look at us curiously (especially at Carol).

The security of the expedition is in danger: at 20:55 we decide, after grueling doubts and deliberations, to carry on to the next rest area (see details in text).

21:00 Departure.

21:03 Mâconnais mountains.

21:07 Sign: "Mâconnais Vineyards."

We don't see them anywhere. On the other hand there are cows.

21:09 Stop: AIRE DE MÂCON ST. ALBAN.

"Relais de Bourgogne" hotel.

Dinner: spaghetti "al sugo", Morvan cheese, coffee.
(In Fafner, we're not up for gastronomical luxuries
today).

At 7:26 we arrive at the Jugy rest area and decide to explore and leave it behind as quickly as possible. Our day doesn't worry us much; according to the map, our next rest stop is right in the middle of nature, and we are cheerfully looking forward to settling down in one of those big rest areas that allow cars to go into the woods, and where it will be possible for us to spend a long day hidden from indiscreet eyes and the sun, which is getting hotter and hotter.

A helicopter flies past very low, and we don't pay it much attention. Had they announced our decision not to stay in Jugy by radio, an intention easy enough to guess at if only because we hadn't raised the expandable roof?

Surprising orography at the Jugy rest area.

From the distance, the dragon envies el Lobo, who's found a bit of shade (Farges rest area).

We arrive at the Farges rest area at 7:46. Not only is it not in the woods, but it hardly has any shade at all and stretches along right up against the freeway. When two Argentines arrive and settle down to drink maté very close to us, it becomes obvious the enemy has decided to adopt more audacious methods. Are they confident the Argentines will be better able than their predecessors to decipher the true secret of this dialogue-made-journey? Two weeks have gone by now, and we imagine, not without certain mischievous pleasure, their long wait and disappointment to discover that Paris–Marseille is nothing more than Paris–Marseille, and that furthermore the police have not intervened to expel these two lunatics from the freeway. Until now, no witness has been able to inform them of any meetings of bearded revolutionaries in the middle of the night, and the only visitors Fafner has received so far have been highly respectable people who have only left us provisions, cherries, and two unexpected bottles of wine. I can imagine the conversations between the boss and his agents at the end of each day:

– Nothing, boss.

– What the hell do you mean, nothing? Are they or are they not still on the autoroute?

– Yes, boss.

– But what the hell are they *doing* there?

– Just what they said they would. Writing a book.

– Fuck the bastards. A book? On the autoroute? And you expect me to believe that?

– Well, you know.

– I know they are nuts, but nobody's *that* crazy! Get your ass back down there and find out what's really going on!

– Boss, about the trash cans . . .

Around about eight-thirty the catastrophes begin, threatening us to such an extent that we must make the decision (oh reader, by now our accomplice, we beg your comprehension!) to break the rules of the game not once but twice. A truck approximately the same colour as the highway services ones, but which in fact belongs to a car rental company as can be seen by an inscription in tiny letters, comes to park right behind Fafner. Two "workers" get out of it, soon joined by the occupants of a second truck (belonging to a swimming pool company), which pulls in behind the first, and out of which the occupants remove with much effort a mysterious machine that will not be used all day.

It's not so much that the noise bothers us (was that what they were counting on, did they think we were the types that could be frightened off by the thumping of a jackhammer?); in any case we're so close to the freeway that the ensemble turns into a concerto for jackhammer and dozens and dozens of heavy cargo vehicles. No, what worries us is that the workers, if they really are workers, are going to be staying here all day, just like us. As the hours go by we see they've started to look at us increasingly insistently. Our unease grows, especially when we see them spending their time on incomprehensible tasks, like excavating a sort of trench in the pavement in front of the WCs. We settle as best we can, moving all the time to take advantage of the thin shade of one of the lot's few stunted trees. Numerous foremen, workers, trucks, and, towards the end of the afternoon, gendarmes pass by, who don't necessarily seem to be required for the job at hand, whatever it might be. And more and more frequently, one or another of the workers leaves his job and goes to the southern edge of the rest area, where there's no work underway, availing themselves of the opportunity to take a long look inside Fafner on the way by.

Towards five a storm threatens – the workers had left a few minutes earlier – and we take shelter inside the dragon, where we deliberate at length about what behaviour to adopt. Everything in us rebels against the idea of cheating, against any repeal of the rules of the game, but we feel that *their* conduct is beginning to put the expedition in serious danger. At this very moment one of the trucks returns, and the gendarmes go past for the second time in less than an hour. We feel exposed, threatened, naked. And we decide that to prevent them from banishing us from the autoroute this very night, it is necessary to make an exception and go on to the next rest area. (If not, we run the risk of attracting too much attention when spending hours and hours in one or another of the most beautiful rest areas, given that it would be understandable if not very normal on this freeway where speed matters more than anything else, while it doesn't seem possible to explain so easily our prolonged presence in one of the ugliest parking lots of all.)

At the next stop there is a hotel where we feel protected from glances, accusations and tricks, although from the moment we arrive we notice they're trying out a new tactic: dishearten us by way of a direct attack on our finances (Sofitel hotel). But we think that the danger has passed since tomorrow the workers will still be working at the preceding rest stop, where they appear to have begun major works. It is inconceivable that they would just dig a trench in front of the WCs and leave.

But the experience we've just been through has marked us, especially since it's the first time we've gone outside our strict rules by arriving at night at a rest area we weren't meant to get to till the following morning. And nevertheless, we're far from suspecting what is to come; the company should never be underestimated, no matter how deserving they are of our disdain.

In the Mâcon-Saint-Albain hotel, la Osita documents the advantages of civilization.

<u>Breakfast: orange juice, croissants, bread and butter, coffee.</u>

10:35   Departure.

10:42   Stop: AIRE DE SENNECE.

Awful!

Fafner facing: S.S.E.

We get lost — separately — in impassable woods. Sad return to Fafner.

11:00   Departure (see text).

11:02   See the Saône River on our left.

11:10   Stop: AIRE DE CRÈCHE.

Just as awful.

We rush to the only table in the (scant) shade.

<u>Lunch: salad of corn, ham, tomatoes and cheese. Coffee.</u>

17:00   49°C in the sun.

18:48   Departure.

18:53   On the right, the Beaujolais mountains.

18:54   Enter Département du Rhone.

18:56   Stop: AIRE DE DRACE.

"Relais de Beaujolais" restaurant.

We fill up with gasoline, to Fafner's immense delight, who waves his yellow fringes (there follows an incomprehensible phrase: "after waiting in line behind a closet").

Fafner facing: N.

<u>Dinner: Parma ham, *petit salé* with lentils (Julio), steak *haché* with frites (Carol), coffee (in the restaurant).</u>

For the first time, the earplugs are essential during the night.

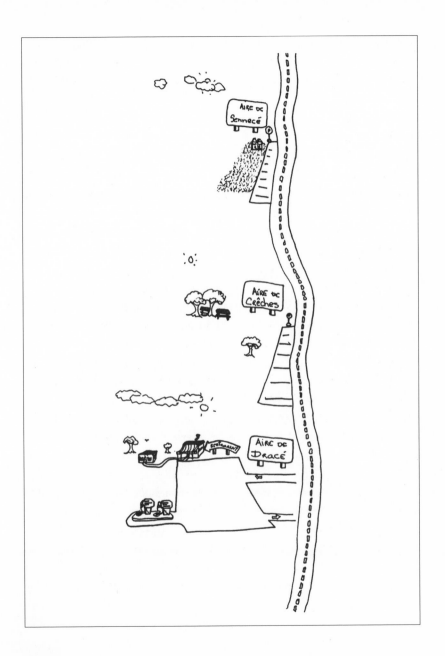

In order to get back on schedule, we'll have to spend the whole day, after leaving the hotel, at the first rest area we come to, which is not too badly situated, according to the map of the autoroute, being right in the middle of a green zone. (It will have been noticed that our optimism frequently runs counter to any effects of pragmatism.) And so we leave Aire de Mâcon-Saint-Alban at about ten-thirty, after a long night and an excellent breakfast, and at about quarter to eleven arrive at Aire de Sennece, which should be called Sennece-the-Sinister, for there is not a single tree, or a bush, or even a table beneath which to get some shade. At the back of the field, there are some steep trails leading towards a forest . . . I decide to take on the mission of exploring them while Julio handles the roof and refrigerator, since we have to install ourselves as best we can until tomorrow morning, and within an hour or two the temperature will reach at least fifty degrees inside Fafner. The climb is more difficult than I thought, and the paths very precarious. I explore as well as possible the woods, full of thorns, ditches and leaves that irritate the skin to such an extent that I return looking like I've caught the measles. Meanwhile Julio has been worried by my absence and gone off to look for me but on the other side.

When I return to our dragon, what – horror and damnation – should I see? The same truck as the day before, that has stopped once more right behind Fafner. Followed by the other truck, both occupied by the same workmen, foremen, engineers, etc., as the day before. And who begin to look at us in a funny way that has nothing funny about it given the circumstances. This time our deliberations are immediate: we scram. If they realize that just like yesterday we're going to spend the whole day where they're working, we've had it. Especially when it's more than evident that our sojourn has nothing to do with the beauty of the rest areas. And since having advanced immediately from one rest area to the next, we find we are a day ahead of our plan, we decide that it would be ridiculous to mark time waiting to get back on track. So we decide to gain a whole day, sure that this way we'll get beyond the reach of the orange ants who – we saw them working yesterday and whatever they're doing seems to take a whole day for each rest area – shouldn't get to the next rest area until tomorrow, when we'll have already left it. That's what we tell ourselves at least, but we have been mistaken before, and quite frequently . . .

At 11:10 then, we arrive at Aire de Crèches, another horror in this region where horrors abound, but we discover a table in the shade and set up to spend the day. It's not ideal, although we are sheltered, even if the helicopters and planes we've seen these last few days continue to fly low above us. Sure that we've escaped, we get out the whisky bottle to celebrate. But, as they say in detective novels, we choke on the first sip. This is when the truck appears, and parks right behind Fafner. This is serious, and there's no way to kid ourselves. We must decide, and quickly, a line of conduct that will save us from this fucking peril. By this stage, and now that they've put their cards on the table, it's Us or Them.

In certain circumstances, the only possible defence is an attack. We realize that the only way to hide the truth (for obviously we cannot tell them that in order to write our Paris–Marseille we've been living on the autoroute since the 23rd of May; they'd think us crazy, suspicious, or worse, and besides, it's illegal) consists in taking immediate action, given that they're looking at us more and more openly, in groups of two or three, and those looks are immediately followed by conversations between them in low voices. The only possibility is to present the truth in such a way that they won't be able to imagine it is what it really is.

And the easiest way to carry this off is for me to turn into Mata Hari, taking advantage for a start of the youngest of the workers, whose glances, yesterday, were not simply those of espionage, at least the official kind. Ostensibly then, while my victim rests in the company of a colleague beneath the shade of another tree, I walk past once and then again with camera in hand and a concentrated expression on my face. To further convince them of my professionalism, I ceaselessly change lenses, check the height of the sun, crouch down and assume almost lascivious positions to take photos I could easily have taken standing up like any normal person. When they get up to go back to work, I approach the youngest, forcing myself to hide my trembling, as the reader can easily imagine. Will I be successful? Won't I give myself away? As if that weren't enough, it's the first time I've ever approached a handsome, well-built young stranger to ask if he'll let me take his photo.

"Hello," I say in a voice that suddenly takes on an indefinable foreign accent. "I think you've been following us since yesterday."

"Yes," he says, looking worried and happy at the same time. Quick, gain some ground before his workmate, an older man, finishes rinsing out his glass and putting the lid on the bottle.

"We're doing a book about the autoroute," I say all at once.

"Oh?"

You can tell he wasn't expecting that.

"Yes, that's why we spend so much time in the rest areas. These days we're on the autoroute almost all the time."

"Is it that interesting?"

(Does he forget that he too, it would appear, is on the autoroute every day? Or have they recruited people from the neighbouring countryside?)

"Oh yes, you see lots of things when you stay here a little longer than usual. Would you mind (here he comes, his workmate approaching, smiling at me mistrustfully) if I took your photo? We're trying to document as much as possible."

"Of course not," says the young man, taking the end of a string the other end of which is in the hand of his mate. "How's this?"

It's more than I'd hoped for.

Carol, Mata-Hari of the freeway, decides to confront the enemy under the pretext of photography.

To convince the enemy, Julio pretends to be writing at full speed, something which always inspires respect.

"That's perfect. And what are you people doing here?"

"Oh," he says with a frank smile this time. "We're levelling the edges for ramps, so the WCs will be accessible to people in wheelchairs."

And all this explains why we sit down to type furiously, interrupted every once in a while by the workers – there are many now – who come to ask us questions and who have adopted us, in order to show them that we're writing a book about the autoroute in order that they won't suspect what we're really doing: writing a book about the autoroute.

(P.S. The only manifestation of hostility from the one who is perhaps the real representative of the company: a man armed with a type of spear, who at one moment comes over and viciously stabs the potato chip packet that Julio has left on the ground almost beneath his feet.)

A resounding, though precarious, success.
The danger past, Carol takes a well-earned rest . . .

. . . . and Julio finally puts his typewriter away.

LETTERS FROM A MOTHER (III)

Savigny-sur-Orge, Monday, 7 June

My dear Eusèbe,

Evidently in this life one can never count on the plans one makes. You'd think fate does it on purpose to spoil them straightaway. In the same way you think you know the people you've lived with for so many years, and then suddenly you find out you know nothing about them, when it's already too late to ask questions.

Poor Héloïse died in her sleep last Tuesday. It's a blessing, really, though it still pains us. According to the doctors, she could have gone on for years. In the state she was in, what good could there have been in that? Maybe, even if she didn't seem to be aware of anything, she knew what was happening when they took her to Joigny. I want to believe that she somehow felt the time had come to let herself go gently. Your father says I'm imagining things. Be that as it may, we went to Joigny as soon as we heard what had happened. There's no one but us to take care of things, after all. The nuns have been very kind. One of them gave me a letter saying that Héloïse had it in her hand when she arrived, and seemed to request that they give it to us after her death. And then, my dear, I had the surprise of my life. I would have liked to wake up poor Héloïse, all white there in her bed, so she could explain.

In the first place, she demands to be buried in Valence, and furthermore next to her husband, well, you know as well as I do that a more maidenly old maid than Héloïse wouldn't be easy to find in this world. And that's not all. She asks that we advise her son of her death, and that we hand over to him another sealed envelope, which was inside the first one. I'd already planned to have the funeral in Ury, where she lived for her whole life as far as I know, and your father agreed that this was no more than a batty old lady's nonsense. I could have sworn that aunt Héloïse had never lived further away than Dijon. As for having a husband and even a son, I think that would at least have been known. Oh, if only you'd been there, you who've studied and who knows how to look at things more logically than I do! Your father said that none of that had any importance, and there was nothing to do other than what was planned, the funeral in Ury and all the rest. But I thought that final requests had to be respected no matter what, and we should at least try to find out if that M. Blanc exists. Your father told me my reading was going to my head and retirement wasn't doing me any good. But I said we at least had to try. After all maybe it's him who has a sclerosis of the brain from not doing anything, not to mention the amount he drinks.

With all that and the nuns who were trying to calm us down a little because after all they have a lot of patients and they didn't want them to find out about Héloïse's death, wouldn't be very good for their peace of mind, you understand. They advised us to go home and sleep on it until the next day, and in the meantime Héloïse could stay there in the chapel of rest. Since I thought she would have thought this a good idea, I said yes and I'll spare you the details of the trip home.

Anyway, I consulted with Anne-Marie and Jacqueline, although they're from another branch of the family. They were both in agreement with me that one should never go against someone's last wishes. Your father insisted that Héloïse would never find out about it, but I told him we can never be sure about such things, although I'm no more of a believer than others. In any case, Anne-Marie came to help me put Héloïse's things in order, and among her papers we found a marriage certificate and a photo of a child. According to the date, we realized he must be about forty years old now. I sent a telegram to the address Héloïse had left, and everything turned out to be true, although as you can imagine I didn't ask many questions. Imagine, telling a perfect stranger that Héloïse had hidden him from us for her whole life! And besides, he already had her space reserved next to her late husband. Her son is taking care of everything, but we'll go to the funeral tomorrow morning anyway.

Meanwhile, since everything seemed to be going ahead without any help from us, we decided to go and spend a couple of days in Dijon, to recover a little. Death always makes an impression, even when you know it's a good thing. So on Saturday we took the autoroute again and . . . do you think senility can start at my age, Eusèbe? It's true your father is no longer the man he used to be, and sometimes I think the same thing is happening to me without my noticing. When we stopped to get gasoline, I

A picnic at the Farges rest area.

got out of the car and went into the service station shop. They sell everything, even pretty earthenware statues. And in there I saw, I swear, that young woman from the camping van, remember? Those people I've run into three or four times on the freeway lately. She's younger than I thought the first time, thirty something, and not at all as tiny as she looks beside her husband, but there wasn't the slightest doubt it was the same person. When I left I saw their vehicle – I'm sure it was the same one – in the woods behind the service station. I wonder, especially now that I've seen her taking photographs, if I shouldn't alert the authorities. You don't think they're planning a robbery?

When I went back to the car, your father announced they had to change the oil. He really chooses the best moment for everything, and I find it hard to understand such a lack of preparation at his age. So I went for a walk through the woods, and I even went close to that strange couple's van. All the curtains were drawn, in the middle of the afternoon. Maybe it's true that the detective novels I've been reading are going to my head, but at my age, you know, a little excitement every once in a

Temptation ever-present. How easy it would be to slip over to the other side!

while is something that does a person good. I approached the van very slowly. Oh, Eusèbe, you don't know how my indiscretion made me blush! What they were doing in there! It turns out they're not married, of that you can be sure! Do you think they're on the run from the police and they think the freeway is a good place to hide? I'm sure it's not allowed . . .

Your father told me I'd imagined it all, and that it's absolutely impossible that it's the same couple. He says there's quite a few of those little trucks on the road. He might be right, but I don't believe him.

Anyway, I'm boring you with my old lady's stories. I ordered flowers in your name for the funeral; especially given the circumstances, we have to show that she had a real family in any case.

Anne-Marie has told me that there are very pretty girls in Canada. I beg you, Eusèbe, be very careful. Most of all, if you find one you like, don't do anything before introducing her to us. I know customs are different in other countries, and you never know up to what point foreigners can adapt.

Thank you for the postcard. I didn't know they had summer in Canada too. I hope your socks and the scarf will be useful in the fall. Don't hesitate to write if you need anything else.

I send you a hug, and I hope your work isn't too tiring. Even though I could never understand why you've chosen to work with crazy people when there are so many sane ones who also need doctors.

Maman

(to be continued)

One believes oneself safe, protected, hidden in the deep green aquarium of the woods; far away runs the shuddering snake of the midday freeway, its moving scales blue, red, black, Renault, grey, Mercedes, silver, green, Talbot. It doesn't matter much, we know by now that the apparent protagonist of the exploration has become an insignificant extra who we only see for a few minutes each day, in two quick stretches that return us each time to the depths of the trees, or, in the worst cases, to the anodyne beach of cement and metal where Esso, Antar, Elf and other idols with equally absurd names await their poor disciples in the course of their smelly and repetitious ceremonies.

But one thinks oneself safe and that's not always the case, although with the skill that now epitomizes us, we've anchored Fafner in the most

Nightfall at l'Aire de Dracé rest area.

The chain on the left, but anyone could pass through on the right (theme of temptation).

Hope it doesn't rain!

secluded, fragrant and shady corner of the parking lot. Barely have we set up the Florid Horrors, barely have we taken out our books, notebooks, cigarettes and drinks, when an enthusiastic stirring in the bushes directs itself our way and, after a moment's fright, we receive on our hands and legs the affectionate assault of a Saint Bernard or the rather interested effusions of a collie. The first impression of being victims of some wild animal having passed, we share out bread, cuddles, fraternity, and the dogs disappear after one last show of perfectly unwarranted, and entirely charming, affection.

They set them free for five minutes, sometimes for half an hour, from those incomprehensible moving prisons accepted with resignation or fury, and their behaviour in the rest stops demonstrates the joy of liberty in its most tumultuous form: running, lifting their leg five or six times not to use up the pleasure on just one tree trunk when there are so many and so much variety, sniffing everything sniffable and finally heading for whoever possesses the eminent virtue of having a sandwich in their hand or some slices of salami on the table. Dogs on the freeway aren't the slightest bit hungry; asking for something is just a courteous pretext to strike up a friendship and forget for a moment the prison that awaits them and from which they try to get away, in spite of the whistles calling them that are like the bourgeois title of ownership over dogs and sometimes wives. They come to us because all dogs know very well which people love dogs, and because an extra mouthful adds to the happiness of the woods among the diverse wilderness episodes punctuating their brief interval out of jail.

There are those big or dumb ones who run around a little lost – their masters have settled down to eat and chat and don't pay them any mind – and then we have to help them, like a couple of days ago with that huge dog of indefinable lineage who, liberated from a little van not much bigger than he was, looked at us with boundless disconcertion when he discovered that the water faucet beside the WCs was obviously a faucet but it didn't give him a drop, despite his offering his entire muzzle, which was quite a lot of muzzle, and seemed to be waiting for the faucet to respond as it should have done if not for its innate inability to communicate with the canine world. It was

Carol who went to help him and earned great tail-waggings of gratitude and wet kisses, but it's almost always them who come to help us, to show us we're not alone, surrounded by those owners of dogs who wander in distant and withdrawn orbits, being so careful of their cars and so careless of life, under the pretext of vacations and rest.

Since children are the same as dogs, luckily, we get along well with them too, because they respond to greetings, they're glad that we're glad to see them, and although their owners don't allow them anywhere near as much freedom as they do their dogs, they often manage to escape and get a few metres into the woods before a mother or a grandfather produces the bellow of alarm and threat and hastens to look for them with an affectionate smile, behind which there are almost always thirty-two teeth in full view. But they can usually find a way to enjoy their brief slice of freedom, just like the dogs. This afternoon, for example, I saw in the distance some refined parents giving their four-year-old son the necessary instructions so that he'd get away from the too-exposed field and go and pee in the trees. The child discovered me sitting in the shade of a holly oak and his first reaction seemed to be uncertainty, followed by a pause during which he appeared to be studying me with that air of deep gravity they assume when preparing to make any value judgement, and then he dropped his drawers without taking his eyes off me, took a firm hold and gave in to the pleasure of any *Manneken Pis*, as if my company rescued him from all the recommendations of modesty and in a way he was peeing on his father's shoes, something I hope he actually will do in a few years' time.

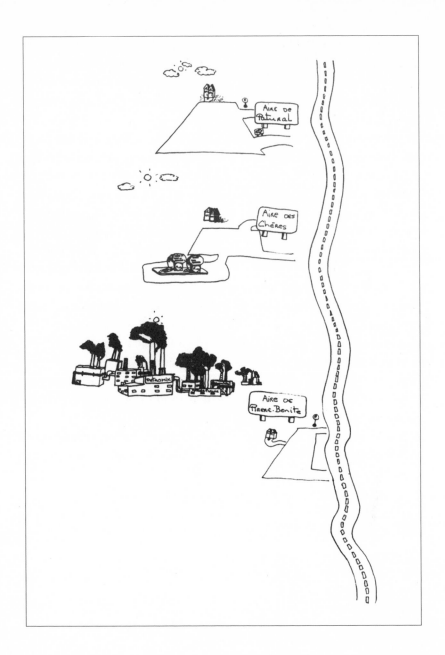

8:00   25°C.

Breakfast: orange juice, croissants, bread and butter, coffee.

8:55 Departure.

9:00 Sign: "Beaujolais Vineyards", but the vines are still invisible.

9:03 Stop: AIRE DE PATUREL.

Fafner facing: S.

10:10 A sign that explorers of old like Christopher Columbus would understand very well: a seagull flies over our heads, lands a few metres from us, and takes flight again. Fafner turns into a tree to give us a little shade. 49°C.

Lunch: salad of tuna, tomatoes and onions. Apricots in syrup, coffee.

15:58 Departure.

16:04 Toll booth: 133 francs. We apologize for having "lost" our ticket and everything is fine, although the employee notes down Fafner's license number.

16:12 Stop: AIRE DE CHÈRES.

Gas station, bare pavement, but we manage to find a pinch of shade.

Fafner facing: E.

Dinner: fried bananas with ham and eggs, coffee.

LETTERS FROM A MOTHER (IV)

Savigny-sur-Orge, Monday, 10 June, 1982

My dear son,
Oh, if only you could have been at Aunt Héloïse's funeral, you would not have believed your eyes! At least half the city of Valence was there. Many elderly people, but, well, I think you'll know what I'm trying to say. People who didn't give the impression of being there because they'd been given a few hours or the whole day off. On the contrary, you could see that each one of them had their own life, and if they were there it was because they considered it their duty. I don't know how to describe what I felt, Eusèbe. Not to mention that I couldn't see most of those present very

The torment of Tantalus at the Paturel rest area. While on our side the sun is merciless, those travelling from Marseille to Paris settle into a place fit for kings . . .

. . . and not even a shred of pity for us, who must shelter in the slim strand of shade that Fafner generously offers.

clearly because my wet handkerchief blurred my vision, and the smell of the flowers made my head spin as well. But my head was already spinning: What if we'd made a mistake, Eusèbe? What if there'd been a misunderstanding somewhere and our Héloïse was not at all the person to whom all these people were paying their last respects? The very idea makes my blood run cold. But it's still harder to believe there wasn't some sort of mix-up. The worst thing was that we almost seemed to be the poor relations there. We hadn't really gone to much expense since we had to make the trip and everything, and besides we thought the ceremony would be quite small. As for the alleged son and his wife – on the telephone he had the voice of a married man, and besides I said to myself that a bachelor wouldn't offer to take care of everything – I couldn't bring myself to ask too many questions, as you can imagine, since as well as glancing askance at us the way they were (your father says I imagined it all, that no one was paying any attention to us, busy as they were crying, drying their eyes and listening to the priest, who seemed around about your age, and with a very lovely voice of the kind that doesn't let you nod off), as well as looking down on us – the flowers we'd ordered, two bouquets, well, Eusèbe, they couldn't even be seen, and believe me that if I could do it again I'd order bigger ones – oh no, I wasn't about to confess that we knew nothing of the Héloïse that everyone there was mourning, you see what a spectacle we would have made of ourselves?

Anyway, it's all over now. I don't know how to explain it to you, it's as if poor Héloïse had been taken away from us twice, now in the ground for eternity under a name we'd never heard mentioned until a week ago, and in a city I could have sworn she'd never known. The worst thing is there's not the slightest doubt. The young M. Blanc received us in his house before the ceremony, to offer us a drink. We were very thirsty, but your father could have abstained from filling up his glass four times in a row. He showed us photos from his childhood, and there was no doubt that the person who held him on her lap was Héloïse. Naturally, I pretended to know all about it, because the opposite would have given him a bad impression of his barely dead mother, don't you think?

But at least in all this, Eusèbe, I'm not the only one implicated, it's a story I don't understand at all but that, and this is certain, is objective. You know me, if there's one quality I always prided myself on it was my objectivity. How can we not believe

Lobo: How many photos are you going to take of me writing?
Osita: Lots. We have to convince the reader of the seriousness of our scientific labour.

in what we see, unless you're going to disregard the evidence before your own eyes, and you know that's not the case with me, even if what happened a week or two ago perturbs me enough that I call everything, absolutely everything, into question, Eusèbe? I didn't know that at my age so many certainties could come tumbling down like a house of cards, and that leads me to ask myself many questions about what had happened before. You're too young to understand very well the effect of such a thought at my age. I don't think they're what you'd call constructive doubts: I'm calling everything into question, I even went to have my sight tested, and I know it's fine. I didn't say anything to your father, he would have been more than happy to tell me my eyesight was failing, supposing it had ever been good. It makes me think what frightens me doesn't only come from my eyes. On the other hand, I know Héloïse's sad end has upset me very much. But that doesn't explain, from my point of view, why every time I travel on the autoroute I see that same couple, as if they lived there, simply coming and going at the pace of . . . well, at a walking pace. After all, it's been quite a while since the first time I saw them, and they're not even at Lyon yet.

I have to interrupt this letter, because your father needs the table to do his accounts (what of, I wonder?), but I'll continue it later. You are perhaps the only one who not only won't laugh at me, but also who might be able to give me explanations, whether from their point of view, or mine.

You know, deep down I almost like to think that Héloïse lived a full, happy life, even if we never knew.

Much love,

Maman

(to be continued)

WHERE FINALLY, AND IT WAS ABOUT TIME,
WE SPEAK OF TRUCKS, WHICH HAVEN'T STOPPED
GOING BY SINCE THE BEGINNING, AND
INVESTIGATE THEIR NOT ALWAYS OBVIOUS REASONS
FOR BEING AND FOR BEING THERE

Up till now we've always been David against Goliath: What can a Renault 5, or even a tremendous Porsche, do when a tractor-trailer precedes it, and another follows ten metres behind and sticks its enormous threatening giant's face in the rear-view mirror, while a third overtakes, making space itself tremble and letting out horrendous snorts? This is how users of the freeway soon develop a complex little studied by Freud, acute truckophobia, which can only be cured by buying a truck to join the enemy's ranks (this is known as transference in psychoanalytic terms) or by taking the train.

We were always in the middle, because Fafner isn't a "heavyweight" but nor is he an ordinary car; from behind his wheel you overlook a wider and more agreeable landscape than when you travel with your backside brushing the ground like in the latest cars, and furthermore the dragon has his allure and inspires respect in the smaller ones and sometimes in the big ones, because the trucks tend to look upon him like a nice little brother and don't bully him like they enjoy doing to the fleas and cockroaches that barely reach their knees. In any case, when we set out on the expedition we had our usual qualms about trucks, and in the early days we tended to avoid them on the roads and in the rest areas. An ingenuous apprenticeship, from which we've now emerged, to enter into the great transport family, which we are now studying very closely and with all due attention and affection.

Dogs can feel important (it's about time) at the Chères rest area.

Chères rest area, where nothing is lacking, except beauty.

And yet, some little trees take us in so that Fafner won't explode like a bubble in the Sahara.

But, of course, there are trucks and there are trucks, and we are sensitive to the qualitative differences, though not the quantitative since they all tend to be enormous. You need only about ten minutes on the freeway to discover the fundamental division: while some trucks openly exhibit their specialty and name or brand of the owner, always adding the location of their head office, others keep these secret. For every so many trucks transporting furniture, horses, fruit juice, gasoline or turrón from Spain, one goes by wrapped in a waterproofed tarpaulin, almost always grey or dark green, making it impossible to tell what it's carrying. This category troubles us, and when we encounter one in a rest area, we study its exponents with close attention, walk all the way around it pretending to stretch our legs, but up till now we've had to be content with the discovery that they have license plates and countries of origin just like all the rest.

What are these always rather sinister, always vaguely threatening trucks carrying? I don't think this autoroute forms part of an arms-trading circuit, nor that the fact of hiding the nature of their cargo saves these trucks from police or customs controls, quite the contrary. It won't do, then, to imagine that they're coming and going from Bulgaria to Paris or from Stockholm to Naples carrying missiles or helicopters; of course, we exclude other explosive cargoes, such as heroin or ginseng roots, for obvious reasons of volume. Why then the secret, why do these trucks resemble certain suburban houses that, with nothing to distinguish them in appearance from those surrounding them, give the impression of being somehow prowled around, somehow inhabited by beings who aren't like those in the other houses? Why, to say it bravely, do they frighten us so?

Carol tends to imagine shameful shipments, that no transport company would be brave enough to proclaim with a sign like the ones cheerfully carrying beer or pigs. She has ventured the opinion that some of them could be transporting cornmeal, tapioca, hair removal cream or no-name noodles, things you can't really announce publicly without blushing. I agree with her that no one would declare with too much pride that they're driving a load of safety pins or bibs. Her point of view strikes me as worthy of consideration and I respect it, contenting myself by imagining less commercial things that under certain circumstances and contexts require discreet transportation; so I think perhaps a rainy country has secretly sold a cloud to a dry country, or that the members of a dissolute club in Oslo have bought from the Yugoslavs a shipment of socialist vibrators, which it seems are more titillating than those from Hamburg or the rue Saint-Denis. And mightn't it be that this second truck wrapped in black canvas, that follows so closely behind the first, is importing a hundred experts in the use of said implements? You're not going to explain that in metre-high letters.

I have other hypotheses: one of those trucks might be transporting a shipment of obese Dutchmen destined for the dietary experiments of an institute in Milan, or vice versa; how can you let eighty fat men out at once at a rest area? I also think of a consignment of rubber gloves, which always evoke disturbing thoughts . . . But the extreme hypothesis, which we both

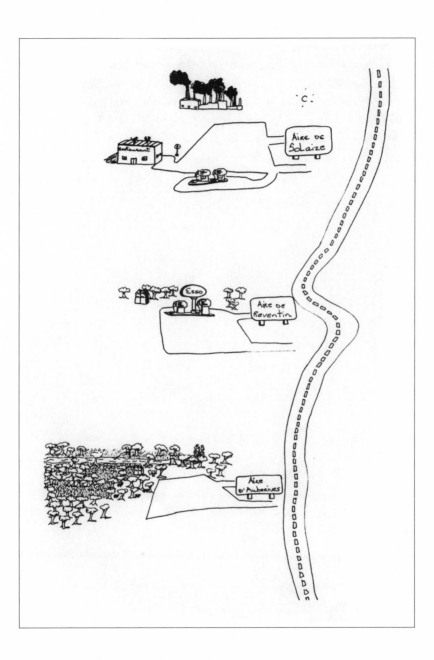

227

agree on without plucking up the courage to believe in too much, is that all those trucks are *empty*, and that they belong to a Scottish eccentric who amuses himself by making them come and go all over the place and receiving weekly reports on the faces of the customs agents when they open them; obviously it's a pastime that must cost millions, but since we're dealing with a Scot, the supreme eccentricity lies precisely in that fact.

ONE TRUCK AMONG MANY

The ghastly bare and sun-drenched rest stop is almost empty, and the truck from Castellón de la Plana stops in front of Fafner, whose inhabitants are engaged in washing the dishes after having consumed a particularly accomplished (by the manufacturer) *nasi-goring*. The truck driver gets out to wash his hands, as we all say in these hospitable parts, and he looks like such a nice fellow that I approach and speak to him in Spanish, knowing that it's like a gift, something he's going to like. And he likes it, of course, and we chat for a while. I learned a long time ago that in opening one of these conversations it's stupid to talk about the weather or the temperature because

We'll never understand how this collection of horrors can answer to the name of Pierre-Bénite.

they're subjects that fly no higher than chickens; it's much more interesting to immediately touch on one's profession, and so I tell him that his job must be a hard slog and all, but in my opinion it gives one more freedom than working for the post office or the Banco España.

"True," he says, "it's good for bachelors."

"Oh. I see. You . . ."

"Well, I've just had a baby girl two days ago in Málaga."

"Wow, congratulations. And everything's fine?"

"Yes," he tells me with a mixture of joy and frustration, "but you see, we thought it would be in ten days time, when I'd be there, and damn it if the little one hasn't beaten us to it."

I congratulate him again, and we say goodbye, since I can see he's anxious to get back on the road and arrive as soon as possible, but first he says he wants to say hello to Carol and he goes over to Fafner to shake her hand and tell the story again. He's suddenly lit up with happiness, he climbs up into his cab and disappears into the distance, maybe thinking that now there are two people who know about the baby girl too, two strangers who shared his joy at any old stop in the world and in life.

<u>Breakfast: croissants, coffee.</u>

10:02   52°C.

10:15   Departure.

10:20   Sign: LYON.

10:22   Exit sign: P-PORTE DE LYON.

We know you have to leave the autoroute to get to this rest area, and we avoid falling into the trap.

10:23   We see a monkey squashed on the road.

10:23 & 10:30   Lyon visible.

10:25   First sign for MARSEILLE.

10:27   First traffic jam since Paris.

10:34   334 kilometres to Marseille.

10:40   We slowly enter the tunnel.

10:50   We come out of the tunnel.

10:51   Another tunnel.

10:52   End of tunnel.

10:56   Stop: AIRE DE PIERRE-BÉNITE.

Fafner facing: S.S.W.

Gasoline, shop, picnic tables, view of petroleum refineries. A horrendous racket.

11:06   Departure.

11:12   Stop: AIRE DE SOLAIRE.

Horror of horrors. But there's a buffet.

<u>Lunch: chicken with frites for one, cold chicken, tomatoes and salad for the other, crème-dessert for both.</u>

15:00   In the end we discover a secret little nook, right near the exit, where there is a little shade. We move there, for Fafner can't stand it anymore in the over-heated cement desert under a furious sun (56°C).

17:00 39°C in the shade.

17:02 Intervention by the "company"? The tanker-truck...

(this note of Carol's is incomprehensible).

Showers! We share them with the truckers.

Dinner: crudités, egg salad for one, Parma ham for the other, coffee.

21:30 25°C.

There is a rather atheistic book attributed to Mirabeau, entitled, I believe, *Erotica Biblion*, which in the Catalan edition I read as a child [sic] was rudely turned into *Pornography in the Bible*. Why not now think of a *Parking Lot Erotica*? We've spent too much time in this all-man's-land not to have sensed its sensual aura, the privileged parenthesis that closes on both sides of French soil to create this interminable eight-hundred-kilometre-long vein, this sinuous sex of man and of woman slipping and opening through mountains and plains, giving and taking in a coming and going that never stops for a moment, infinite orgasm from Porte d'Orléans to the final spasm

Even the beer caps contribute to the monstrosity of Pierre-Bénite.

of a Marseille born of Phoenician love and Hellenic refinement, privileged receptacle for the culmination of a pleasure that began in so many rest areas, in so many deep nights.

I'm speaking for us, for la Osita and myself, but also for much that we discern in the parking lots, where everything appears so functional and mechanical when you only look for that or *are* that. The tourists and businessmen with their eyes glued to the freeway I'll let pass without comment, mouths with tastes for badly chewed sandwiches; I'll let them pass because the ceremonies, chances, encounters and coronations operate in another dimension, and especially in the trucks, mobile enclosures of virtually ever-present, almost always concealed sensuality. From the first days we learned to recognize them: they arrive with a snort that might be part of the secret codes of the road, a password to others, availability. As evening closes in, they begin to park one behind the other or parallel to each other; a furtive traffic of silhouettes, of dialogues, weaves through the advancing shadows. Among them, Fafner enjoys the respect a little truck deserves: there are hands that rise in a friendly greeting, conspiratorial smiles. The big rest areas with service stations, a shop and almost always a restaurant see a small, ephemeral, changing city grow up each night that will only exist once, to be replaced by a similar but different one the next day. Suddenly the city is complete, and it's the most international city in the world, with Bulgarian, French, German, Spanish, Greek, Belgian houses, long houses with inscriptions or huge canvasses beneath which mystery shelters; houses with many rooms, with kitchens, bathrooms, television, lights; houses where a couple or a man or a woman live alone, sometimes dogs, sometimes children, and always camping stoves, bottles of wine and beer, aromas of soup or frites.

In Paris, seeing a woman driving a heavy cargo vehicle every once in a while still provokes an instant surprised reaction in men, quickly concealed, as if embarrassed that they still consider it transgression, even insolence. On the freeway that feeling is almost admiring, to see a monster of who-knows-how-many-tons pull up, with its enormous trailer, and suddenly a glimpse of blonde above the steering wheel, white arms and a colourful blouse, see a woman climb down, resolute and sure, much more womanly than many women, who kicks the tires, checks the latches and tension of the tarpaulin, fills a water bottle and goes into the WC to emerge again with a freshly washed face, shaking out her hair, taking pleasure in the brief walk. Almost always she'll be accompanied by a big dog, gentle and playful but perhaps quite different inside the cab. In the majority of cases a second truck from the same company arrives shortly after, a man climbs down from it and the couple is complete for the stop, for the night. Sometimes it's two men; so far we've never seen two women.

The haphazard construction of the phantasmagoric city leads us to witness some chance encounters, which also form part of the code, like a couple of days ago when we saw the pair of young truck drivers who were talking in a way that could only be fragmentary, based on the smiles and gestures and joy of hitting it off. She drove a Swedish truck, he was French; they undoubtedly had a vocabulary of fifty English words betweeen them, but all the same they'd decided to take photos, all the same they visited each other in their respective cabs to open a beer or a can of something. All this lasted a very short while, a tyrannical schedule prevented them from forming part of the nocturnal city, unless they'd decided to meet again at the next more congenial rest stop (this one was not and Fafner vegetated there in accordance with the law of the expedition, with the air of a sad mushroom which he passed to us).

We saw the young truckers climb up to their command posts; she left first with a last wave, and he followed her, after smiling at us as if understanding that we couldn't choose a better place, or simply because he thought we were stupid. We stayed reflecting on that ephemeral encounter that might give them a long night of happiness a bit further on, or perhaps never.

◇　◇　◇　◇

Sometimes we find them already together, already a stable couple inside their cab, like yesterday afternoon's young Germans, who played at climbing in and out of the truck between laughter and bottles of fresh water and

Where one can admire the dragon's artistic talent as he adorns himself with a set of shadows.

a feeling of happiness that filled them with sunlight, as if it were lacking in this damned rest area where two or three stunted, balding trees produced as much shade as a second-hand umbrella, beneath which la Osita and I worked like fiends in order to forget our surroundings, which were practically non-existent. But maybe because of that, because of the overwhelming heat we'd endured, the next rest area seemed like an oasis, with its restaurant (*Le Ralais du Beaujolais*, please take note), its shop with oh-so-necessary provisions at this stage of the expedition, and its interminable parking lot where one after another the houses that would fabricate the phantasmal city for a few hours gradually began arriving.

As tends to happens to us, we'd put Fafner in the worst possible place, which on the one hand was far from the roar of the freeway, but on the other was right beside the exit ramp for vehicles resuming their journey. With the euphoria of a *steak haché pommes frites* (la Osita) and a *petit salé aux lentilles* (el Lobo) washed down with the eponymous wine, we thought it a fitting location and went to bed without more ado. However, going to bed in Fafner is a much easier procedure than getting up, since the bed, once opened, occupies most of the space reserved in the daytime for the vertical or sitting state, not to mention that we'd also gone to bed naked, as is right and proper (are there still people who sleep in pajamas in this world? American movies lead one to suspect there are, but we suppose it must be part of the frustrations of that poor country), and so, getting dressed again in case of emergency is one of the Herculean tasks culpably forgotten by Hesiod and other chroniclers. Once in bed, into which we slip like startled fish / half charged with firelight / half charged with ice, nothing seems horrible enough to us to make us get up and move Fafner, a task that would also require the removal of various bags and bundles as well as taking in the sails, or rather the roof of the dragon, who at this hour raises his yellow crest towards the stars.

Going over scientific observations . . .

. . . leads to raptures that transform el Lobo into Glenn Gould.

Due to all that we stayed where we were, but five minutes later our real suffering began: one after another, trucks and cars and camping vans started arriving, stopped for a moment for some reason beside Fafner, shone their headlights right into the semi-darkness within, and then started their engines again with tremendous roars and explosions to get back onto the freeway. All this, objectively, would have been infernal, and in some way it was, but at the same time the signs were inverted and the mechanical hounding, the gusts of light and the harassment from the trucks on their way or already parked became more and more favourable for the fiestas of the night, for the night in the rest area, for what we'd been discovering bit by bit and now crackled with ourselves in the centre, naked in the changeable aquarium, in the incredible and absurd extraterrestrial capsule, marvelling pilots of a UFO that just touched down amid trucks and entered into this game, which those who lashed us with their lights and turned us into the centre of nocturnal revels of engines and fire could never have suspected.

In this state of weightlessness, in this iridescent bubble that was changing its lights and sounds continuously, we knew that night was the night of our fiesta, that after so many days advancing and exploring we had been accepted by one of the ephemeral cities, that unknowingly the truckers were surrounding us in a ceremony of initiation and recognition, putting in our hands the invisible keys to the phantasmal city, and that at dawn the place would be grey and deserted, that Fafner would wake up like Cinderella on an empty and indifferent stretch of cement. We experience the wonder that so many things horrible in themselves can become wonders for and by ourselves, we accept in a slow, delicious, interminable ceremony all that we have always denied in our lives in stable, petrified cities. Bedouins in a one-night camp, mutants of a few hours, in which loving each other was like doing it in a kaleidoscope, proteiform and fleeing, covered in phosphorescent stars or wrapped in quick bursts of shadow, falling in wells of silence where our murmurs were like yet another caress, until we received the screeching lash of braking like an echo of antediluvian terrors, of megatheria stepping on the bracken of time.

And then we slept, Osita, and well into the morning you kept sleeping, and it was only me who was to see the end of the rest area night, the low sun that turned Fafner's crest into an orange cupola, that slipped in through the lateral curtains to get into bed with us, started to play with your hair, with your breasts, with your eyelashes that always look thicker, always look so much thicker when you're asleep.

I also played this last game before the oranges and coffee and fresh water, a game that comes from childhood and consists of covering up with the sheet, disappearing into those waters of thick air, then while on your back, bending your legs to make a tent, and inside the tent establishing a kingdom and playing in there, thinking that the world is only this, that outside the tent there is nothing, that the kingdom is just the kingdom and all's well in the kingdom and nothing else is necessary. You're sleeping with your back turned to me, giving me your back, as we say in Spanish, and here and now it's so much more than a mere turn of phrase, because your back is bathed in the aquarium light born of the sun filtering through the sheet turned translucent cupola, a sheet with fine green, yellow and red lines that dissolve into luminous dust, gold floating where your body inscribed its darkest gold, bronze and mercury, zones of blue shade, pools and valleys.

I've never desired you more, never has the light trembled so on your skin. You were Lilith, you were Cypris, from the rest area night you were reborn to the sun like the murmurs growing outside, the motors starting up one after another, the noise of the freeway growing with the influx each rest area sends running down it after sleep. I look at you so much, knowing you're going to wake up lost and startled like always, that you won't understand anything, not even the secret tent or my way of looking at you, and that we'll both start the day as usual, smiling at each other and "orange juice!" and looking at each other and "coffee, coffee, gallons of coffee!"

LETTERS FROM A MOTHER (V)

Savigny-sur-Orge, 11 June, 1982

My dear Eusèbe,

Since your father's gone to the doctor, and knowing him as I do, he'll take advantage to dawdle around until dinner time, I have a bit of time to write to you and try to put this story a little more clearly. Well, this obliges me to also tell you some things I would have preferred to keep quiet about, but anyway, at your age, as your father says (although of course he has no idea of what I tell you in my letters) you must be able to look life in the face.

Dragons do not like wind, and Fafner warily observes the indications of crosswinds and dangerous gusts.

A Beethovian stream at l'Aire d'Auberives.

An unexpected swell during the night, demonstrating one of the possible dangers of the expedition.

For the last two or three years we've got out of the habit of taking long trips like we used to when you were young and vacations were still vacations. Your father tends to get exasperated on the road, and travelling many kilometres at a time tires us. That's why we'd decided to go to Valence the night before Aunt Héloïse's funeral, sleep in a hotel and be well-rested for the ceremony. Anyway, it so happened your cousin André chose that exact day to pay us a visit and how could we not invite a relative who arrives at midday to stay for lunch? And there you have them, your father and he launched into tales of tennis and soccer and who knows what else, and of course all this they celebrate with drinks, and I bet you this, and I challenge you that, and another glass is emptied. For all of which we only left the city at five in the afternoon, and I confess I didn't feel at all safe getting into the car with your father. I wouldn't say he was drunk, not exactly, but he'd certainly been drinking. When we reached Mâcon, seeing that his eyes were closing behind the wheel, I insisted we stop at the first hotel, and it almost seemed a miracle when he agreed. Almost immediately we saw a sign for a hotel right on the autoroute. Without a peep of protest, he turned into the rest area and we found one of those stretched-out hotels, you know what I mean, the ones that aren't vertical, and in front of each room is a place for the car. They're called motels, your father informed me. It seems that in the United States all the hotels, or motels, are horizontal. Anyway, it was clean, with a bathroom and everything. I couldn't believe that your father didn't get enraged even about the price, though it has to be said what with the cost of living these days it was fairly reasonable. But obviously fate would have it that your father told me straight away that I mustn't drink a little bottle of fruit juice from the small fridge installed right there in the room, because the prices were highway robbery. He started to wonder whether he shouldn't go into business with Albert Desmoix, you remember him, he had a hardware store on Dufour Street when you were little, to set up a chain of hotels. I didn't think he was serious. In any case, he destroyed all my pleasure when he turned on the television and said: what luck, just in time for the game. You see what I mean, it made me wonder if he hadn't planned the whole thing from the start. In any case, since I couldn't even have a glass of orange juice and he had his famous game of whatever it was, I wasn't going to give him the pleasure of having me stay in the room and put up with sports. I decided to go and eat, because there was a restaurant there and everything. On my way out of the room, I saw quite clearly that there was a red Volkswagen van a little ways away, but it didn't occur to me that it might be them. And nevertheless, believe it or not, Eusèbe, I went into the little restaurant called Le Bistrot, and I swear they were there, enjoying a nice meal like everyone else. I looked at them very closely, I assure you they're real and there's nothing strange about them, except that they look a bit happier than normal people, but that's no reason to judge them. They paid with a Visa card and everything, and they left holding hands. I saw them walk across the big parking lot in the direction of the motel, and after what happened the other day, I prefer to stop that thought right here. Eusèbe, do you think it's possible that these people have not left the freeway since the first time I saw them? I can't say exactly why, but I have the impression they're not going anywhere. But then, what are they doing on the freeway? It's not worth discussing with your father, he'll accuse me of being outlandish again. But this is not the work of my imagination. Besides, if I did have frustrations, I think I would use a different type of . . . how do you call it, projectiles?, instead of this, that really doesn't seem to make any sense. Anyway, a ghost can't pay with a Visa card. (Ah well, since I'd decided to tell you everything, they'd left the receipt on the table and I went over – I'm embarrassed, but now you see how much this story disturbs me – I went to pick it up, to prove that it wasn't all an invention of mine. Of course, I was going to throw it away on my way out. Imagine if I had to explain what I was doing with the receipt from a stranger's Visa card.)

When I think they could have caught me, I don't know how I did it, but I went to look inside the van. I don't really know what to think about the mixture of things I saw: oranges suspended in a net, a bottle of whisky practically on display, a compass, a thermometer, typewriters (yes, there are two, very small ones, and they set them up side by side between the driver's seat and the passenger seat); I saw a little fridge, a pair of binoculars, all sorts of cards and notebooks, as well as a great big radio and cassette player, a bit like the one you dreamed of buying two or three years ago. There was even underwear hanging in one of the little windows.

Anyway, my dear, time goes by and I think I've told you the essence of the matter. I don't understand who these people are, or what they're doing on the freeway. In any case I know I haven't imagined them, and – Jacqueline made me think of this,

Auberives rest area: for those looking for peace . . .

. . . and who want to hear birdsong.

that I should have foreseen from the beginning – this time I wrote down their license number, so if I see them again there will not be the slightest possible doubt remaining. But tell me, Eusèbe, why do you think they're obsessing me to such a degree?

Think of us every once in a while. You know you're the most precious thing we have in this world.

Much love,

Maman

Reading these pages,
has it not occurred to you,
at least once, oh complicit
and patient reader, to wonder whether
we haven't been hidden in some
hotel room in la Villette since
the 23rd of May?

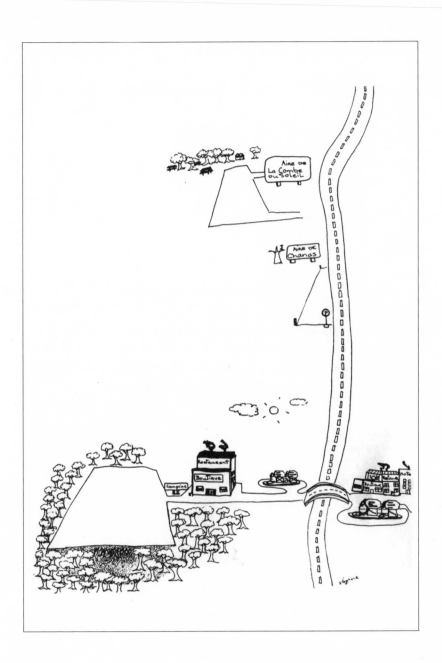

249

<u>Breakfast: orange juice, croissants, jam, coffee.</u>

9:25 Departure.

9:30 Romanesque church on the left.

9:45 Toll booth.

9:47 Stop: AIRE DE REVENTIN.

Exploration without leaving Fafner, since it's raining cats and dogs.

10:00 Underwater departure.

10:02 Stop: AIRE D'AUBERIVES.

Trees, a stream, tables, all far from the freeway.

Fafner facing: S.

<u>Lunch: salami sandwiches. Cheese, coffee.</u>

<u>Dinner: couscous, coffee.</u>

During the night, copious rain. In the morning, looking at what yesterday was a crystal-clear stream trickling over rocks and stones, we see a raging river. The current could have swept us away during the night!

The autoroute is a rose river, along which floats a barely perceptible violet mist, and the cars and trucks pass like ghosts, their deafening noise hushed at night by the fog that softens everything, by the distance between them and us, which delimits the worlds where we live, as if we were not, nor could we ever be, travellers on the same road. Strange silence full of murmurs, broken from time to time by a truck starting up, by the screeching brakes of a train, silence made of sounds and noises and whose existence – in which each one of our gestures participate – confirms in a way that we are where we think we are, that the objective of the trip has been reached, and it's only

At the Combe du Soleil rest area, a girl seems to be performing the dance of a redskin warrior. What happened in the WC?

Auberives: picnic paradise where savage battles rage for possession . . .

. . . of a table, and where the discovery of a free place for lunch is to be savoured.

left for us to say to ourselves, with that smile that perhaps unknowingly means that you'll take another step forward and that I'll find myself again in your arms, that this objective is no more fixed than the rest stops, that we're living the world or the stars more naturally every day.

The freeway is not a straight line but a spiral, our two lives also spirals, and the vertigo of those lines that cross, in the mosaic of the circles and tangents, parallel and intersecting; and only an arbitrary decision – we took it before going down this path, without worrying about its importance – will make us leave one day (happily still distant) the game and the space that defines it.

A grapefruit-coloured moon, heavy like velvet, illuminates the inside of Fafner. Bit by bit our bodies emerge from the invisibility that follows the moment we turn out the lamp. I wait, knowing that from the darkness where I can only just make you out from the heat that rises towards me with a scent of moon, of cinnamon, of musk and chocolate, you'll be reborn again, bit by bit, to the night, to our night that has been luminous since the beginning of the voyage, with an ever-changing light through the curtains on the windows and the mosquito nets on the expandable roof. Your shoulder, first, catches a luminosity that it timidly returns, a twinkling that slowly irradiates the length of your neck, plays in your beard; your face stays dark. That lasts an eternity and we don't move, patient, serene. Bit by bit you brighten, as if your body had spent the day soaking up light that it now frees, prudently, as if not to damage the skin on its way through. It runs the length of your silver arm, reaches your hip, your waist, and from there stretches all the way down your legs. You don't move. Nor do I, but my gaze returns confidently to your face, that face that is now the colour of the golden moon. We are there again, whole, like two bright bodies barely born out of the dark, soon to offer hands, arms, legs, blend again those scents, all those limbs, all those cries.

Much later, I pull back a corner of the curtain and look out the window. As if sheltering against Fafner, who receives him in the most paternal manner possible, a young biker from Bern sleeps on his motorcycle, like a strange creature from another world. Fearful of the rain, he's turned the plastic sheet he carries with him into a great bubble that now protects the machine and its rider. Beneath a tenuous light that comes from far away, he looks like a barely formed angel, a hazy vision through the transparent plastic. He didn't know if Marseille was a great city, or how far away it was, and he explained, rather shyly, that he knew no one in Marseille, with the same tone someone would use to say: "I know no one in the world." But now he's asleep, his head resting on his sleeping bag, his feet on the handle bars, and his teenage face illuminated by a peaceful smile.

Breakfast: orange juice, croissants, madeleines, coffee.

8:00 18°C. Fresh, rainy weather.

13:15 Departure.

13:19 On the right, the Massif Central. Mont Pilat.

13:20 Stop: AIRE DE LA COMBE DU SOLEIL.
Fafner facing: S.W.
A few tables, not much shade for us and none for Fafner.
We decide to tempt fate at the next rest stop.

13:26 Departure.

13:34 Stop: AIRE DE CHANAS.
Lunch: spaghetti, apples, coffee.
Bad luck: there is no shade, no privacy, not even a WC or drinking water: all is asphalt and garbage cans.

16:35 We decide to flee from the Chanas rest area due to circumstances beyond our control: police presence, absence of water, facilities, etc.

16:38 We enter Département de la Drôme.

16:40 Stop: AIRE DE SAINT RAMBERT D'ALBON.
Dinner: crudités, ravioli de Romans.

At the Chanas rest area, the only conspicuous thing is the gendarmes, building.

The dragon looks quite lost in the desolation of l'Aire de Chanas.

DEMEANOR IN THE REST AREAS

For "Dash" and for Raymond Chandler, for obvious reasons.
For Claude-Edmonde Magny who defined his books as
"novels of manners". And for Osvaldo Soriano,
for his friendship.

"Get your hand out of there," I said to Sonia. "You don't want us to crash right in front of the motel."

"And who took my panties off two kilometres back?" asked Sonia, doing as I said.

The parking lot lights cut a small section out of the woods; we pulled off the freeway and I hardly slowed down till we got near the gas pumps; I left them behind, and the car screeched as usual as I braked in front of the motel. Cars and more cars filled the forecourt and it was hard to find a free space. We got out the overnight case and the bag with the drinks. I looked at the motel and counted the cars.

"You're really tired," I said to Sonia. "You're falling asleep on your feet."

"Me? I've never felt less sleepy."

"Nevertheless, you're so tired you can't go on. So much so that you're going to lean on my shoulder, I'll hold you up like this, and when we get inside, your eyes'll be half-closed and you'll be breathing with difficulty."

"But . . ." said Sonia, and did as I said. She did it very well, especially at the moment we approached the blonde who was handing a key to a guy who looked Italian. I put the bags on the floor and took Sonia slowly over to the faded sofa in the lobby; the Italian went to his room and there was no one else left.

I set Sonia down gently; she leaned over and closed her eyes and I went back over to the counter. The blonde looked at me the way she must look at everybody, including flies and cockroaches.

"A room, please," I said unnecessarily.

"I'm sorry, I just gave that gentleman the last one," said the blonde, opening an illustrated magazine and holding it a few centimetres from her bust. She would have had to move it quite a bit to be able to read it without difficulty.

I leaned on the counter, with a gesture of a mountain climber grabbing hold of the only possible thing within reach of his hand.

"Please, put us anywhere, my wife is exhausted. She hasn't been well all day, and we've done . . ."

"I can't invent vacant rooms," the blonde said. "And I can't let you sleep on the sofa, the manager does not allow it."

"We have a very small car, full of stuff. She . . ."

"There's another motel in sixty kilometres."

"Please," I repeated, in a voice that works well when I need it in special circumstances. "It doesn't matter about me but if you could find a space for Sonia, I don't know, a mattress or a sofa somewhere. We'll leave early, won't make any trouble for you."

Sonia's arm slid the length of the sofa and her fingers brushed the carpet. The blonde saw her before looking back at me. This time she really looked at me before speaking, and closed the magazine.

"I can put her in the first aid room," she said. "There's hardly space to move in there because the stretcher's too big for the room, and only one person just barely fits."

It wasn't good news and I kept from looking at Sonia; I was sure she'd wake up indignantly and blow the whole thing. At that very moment a couple who looked truly exhausted turned away before they'd even had a chance to open the door because the blonde was pointing to the NO VACANCIES sign she'd just put up on the counter.

"Thanks so much," I said, "you're doing us a big favour."

The strange impression of sentinels given by the garbage cans.

The blonde handed me a blank registration card and went right over to the sofa, waiting for Sonia to stand up. Without a word, Sonia followed her to a door beside the counter, and before going through it, glanced sideways at me, and I barely had time to raise my hand slightly so she'd understand that things were how they were and that night we wouldn't be able to carry on what had started in the car, what always started in the car before arriving at a motel.

The blonde was back in no time, sent away a Yugoslav or Romanian who wanted to stay the night, and sat down behind her open magazine. But first turned to look at me.

"You can stay there," she pointed at the faded but quite large sofa. "I still have another twenty minutes but then I'm going to sleep and I'll turn out the lights."

"Thank you. Really, thanks so much. Would you like a cigarette?"

"I don't smoke."

I picked up a sports magazine and sat down on the sofa. Football didn't strike me as interesting at that hour, with Sonia on a stretcher and the whole night ahead on a not too comfortable sofa. The blonde was concentrating on her magazine, but after a while opened the side door and disappeared; I thought I heard a man's voice somewhere behind the reception and when she came back I looked at her without too much interest, I simply looked at her and she did the same.

"I always have to tell the cook to go home," she explained unnecessarily. "Seems like the pots and pans amuse him. It's almost midnight and he's still hanging around. When we close here, we close."

She had a key in her hand and went to the entrance carrying the NO VACANCIES sign, which she hung on the door. The lights went out, except for a very weak one behind the counter, leaving me in the dark about the second division results. I put the magazine on the carpet and waited for the blonde to leave before stretching out. I've never liked to be seen lying on a sofa, and the night had only just begun.

The blonde went back behind the counter, put the keys away in one drawer and the magazine in another. Now all that was left was a "good night", which I'd answer with another, and a "thanks again" as an appropriate tip. But you should never get ahead of yourself, because surprises are always waiting in the wings, eager to pounce.

"You're not going to be very comfortable on that sofa," said the blonde. "Come with me."

I'll never know how I made it to the side door almost before she did. She led me down a hallway where there were one or two doors, behind one of which Sonia must have been furious on her stretcher, and then elbowed the first door on the left open. It was a bedroom with an enormous bed, a bar built into the wall, television and wardrobes and armchairs made of light-coloured wood. But it wasn't a motel bedroom, there were bottles and jars on the dresser, a bathroom door at the foot of the bed and open or closed magazines everywhere, ashtrays and lamps and more magazines. The blonde locked the door and stood looking at me.

"You like?"

There were several possible ways to answer; mine was to grasp her by the shoulders, pull her to me and kiss her on the lips, which still seemed to be just finishing the question. We arrived at the bed as if dancing a very close tango, I fell on top of her but she slipped to one side and still kissing we began to take our clothes off. I saw she was like me, only with all her skin out in the open did she feel good in bed.

"There's no hurry," she said when I wanted to run my hands over her from top to bottom. "We've got all night, my husband doesn't get back till seven-thirty."

I heard the information without it mattering to me in the least, the blonde was incandescence itself, eventually seeming in more of a rush than me and giving me almost no time to explore, to search her with fingers and mouth before feeling the arc of her legs and entering live coals, getting tangled up in blonde lianas that crept into my mouth and eyes, feeling bronze-like fingers hitting and stroking me while a broken, panting voice repeated "now, now", asked for "more, more", chose "that's it, like that", until a first withdrawal that didn't last long, whisky from the bar, the discovery, which I refrained from commenting on, that she smoked like a chimney, the itinerary of two hours with interludes of sleep and caresses and more drinks, towards dawn more love, but this time the blonde who turned out to be called Norma didn't allow my preferences, but lay on her side with her back to me, drew me slowly to her and said one of the few things she'd said that night: "Come in very, very slowly, and put your leg on top of mine." I did, of course, although it's not one of the positions I prefer, and Norma began to enjoy it almost immediately, now she trembled from head to toe while letting out a sort of stifled lowing, a hoarse groan that went on and on and was cut off in a sort of reproach when I couldn't contain myself any longer and surrendered to orgasm, unable to prolong that pleasure that I would have liked to keep giving, as any self-respecting man would.

I dreamed of toy trains, of Sonia talking to me about her mom, of a horse race. Norma woke me up rather brusquely and I saw the morning light in the lace curtains.

"Have a quick shower and let's get going," she said. "It's getting late and I have to open."

I wanted to pull her to me and kiss her, but she was already dressed and had a magazine in her hand. I took a shower, of course. Thinking of Sonia, of course. Norma took me to the lobby, opened the door and took care of the first guests who paid and left. I sat down on the sofa to read the Liga results, and I'd got to a weight-lifting championship in the Ukraine when I saw Sonia come in. We told each other we'd slept very well, even though the stretcher, of course, and the sofa, of course. The guests seemed to have reached an agreement to all leave at the same time, but now there was another employee in the lobby with Norma, probably her husband. I paid him for the night, waiting for him to ask me for the room number and the key, but he didn't say anything. We said goodbye the way one does in motels, and the freeway was empty and sunny. That day we did almost four hundred kilometres, without much talking because we both seemed to be tired and all we could do was joke about stretchers and sofas. Luckily there were rooms free in the motel we found at six in the evening, and after having a drink and a bath we looked at each other and it was like always, Sonia pulling off the comforter, undressing, finding each other, intertwining.

We stopped for another drink, went out for dinner and at ten-thirty we were back in bed, reading the papers and having one more drink that was always the penultimate. In those cases there is a hand that slides under the sheet until it finds something it was looking for, another that throws a magazine or a pillow up in the air, another that turns off the light, we're like a happy octopus full of busy tentacles. And as always, it's me who slips down the length of Sonia who's lying face up, kissing her little by little because we're already tired and at the same time we feel the pleasure's not over yet. As always it's me who does this, except this time because Sonia kisses me on the mouth and won't let my face away from hers, kisses me and kisses me, stroking my backside and waist, laughingly struggling against my resistance and holding me to her as she gradually turns onto her side, now she couldn't kiss me but her left hand went over her waist and came looking for something she knew so well, stroking me till I was nearly screaming, she lay right on her side, turned on her side while asking me to come in very slowly, just bit by bit, and to put my leg on top of hers, come into her slowly with my leg on top of hers, as we'd never done before, the way I'd only done with Norma.

At the strategically important Saint-Rambert d'Albon rest area, we feel spied on from above.

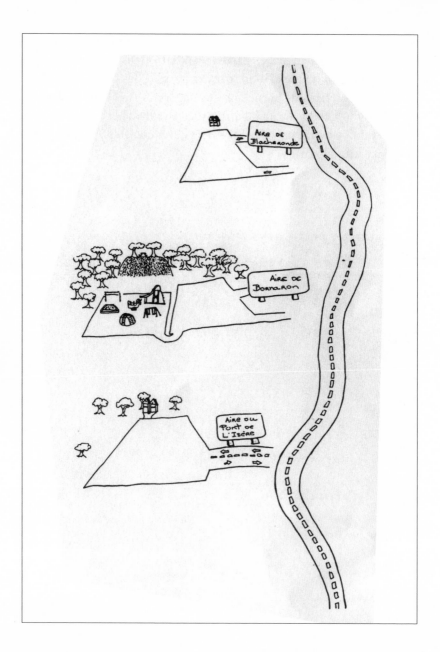

Breakfast: orange juice, madeleines, coffee.
Weather between cool and cold. Cloudy. We set up at a
table to await the second relief mission. The rain forces
us to take shelter inside Fafner.

13:26 Arrival of the lifesavers! Jean Thiercelin and his
son Gilles, and Brynhild Mascret, all loaded with fresh
food, news and affection.

Lunch: sausage from Cucuron, cold meats, *"caillettes"*,
cheeses, cakes, coffee.

18:45 After the whole afternoon with our friends, we see
them off, and depart in our turn.

18:50 Stop: AIRE DE BLANCHERONDE.
Fafner facing: E.

Dinner: cold meats, salad (from the vegetable plot of
Captain Thiercelin), cheese, coffee.

Things began rather badly due to a rain storm worthy of the jungles of Sumatra, which completely spoiled our plans for an official reception in the pre-arranged rest area of Saint-Rambert d'Albon, and which consisted of: 1) table set for lunch beneath the trees, it being understood that said

Aire de Saint-Rambert d'Albon: the second rescue mission arrives loaded with fresh provisions. Jean Thiercelin, Bryhnild Mascret and Gilles Thiercelin check that the explorers have resisted the hardships of the voyage.

lunch would be provided by Jean Thiercelin's relief mission; 2) sun, birds, heat; 3) documentary and celebratory photos of the technical and emotional connections.

Beneath such an emphatic downpour and along with various tourists, among them an agitated group of young French judokas who suddenly lost all their martial demeanor, we fled back to our respective vehicles and there, in a damp and down-in-the-mouth Fafner, we sat down to wait, melancholically eating slices of salami washed down with a glass or two of red wine. It was just starting to clear up as we saw Jean's Volkswagen approaching, and from it he emerged with his son Gilles and Brynhild Mascret, their hands and arms full of bottles, packages, bags, lettuces, roast chickens, tomatoes, peas, oranges, peppers, ice cubes, tins of cream and other provisions aimed at keeping all threat of scurvy at bay, not to mention four bottles of scotch, a drink that in my opinion kills microbes better than any antibiotic.

Everything went well from that moment on; we got out the table and covered it in marvels, told each other all sorts of exciting things, saw planes doing acrobatics as if the municipality of Chanas wanted to associate itself with our festivities, and all this while la Osita and I enjoyed the visit with that feeling common to all explorers who come out of the long tunnel of isolation before entering another, and who savour the delights of an encounter and, while we were at it, the *rôti de porc*, which was a real luxury.

Do expeditions invite wagers? You might think so, considering the famous one that took Phileas Fogg on his dramatic voyage. As far as we're concerned, Jean Thiercelin informed us that his / our friend Vladimir had coldly declared we'd never make it to Marseille, and to back up this statement he gave the following reasons: Unbearable boredom after twenty rest areas / conjugal disputes as a result, which would push the spouses in opposite directions, but in both cases back towards Paris / mechanical,

Bryhnild and Carol celebrate the happy encounter.

nutritional and gastric problems / hunger and thirst caused by poor admin-
istration of provisions, taking into consideration the explorers' considerable
amateurism / irresistible urges to go to the cinema / ditto for a decent bed
/ nostalgia for the metro / ditto for hot showers / ditto for *pommes frites*, as
the expeditionistas would be unable to prepare them / etc.

As a result of this conviction, Vladimir bet Jean a dinner (with us
included, of course, since he likes us very much even if he has no belief in
our abilities). Furious and defiant, Jean took the bet straight away, despite
how much a good dinner for five could cost him if he loses.

"But I know I'm not going to lose," he told us, filling our wine glasses. "I
just have to look at you after twenty days of struggle and valiant progress,
to see your morale's high as hell."

"It most certainly is," la Osita and I chorused.

Our dear Brynhild, who can be a wonderful friend while at the same time
being a doctor and observing us clinically out of the corner of her eye, gave
her unspoken approval, and left us reinvigorated. When we said farewell
as the day drew to a close, we sent Vladimir a message: he will lose the bet,
but we'll spend a lovely evening with him, needless to say he'd take us to
a very decent restaurant. No tinned tuna or hard-boiled eggs for us, after
our thirty-two day ordeal.

Full of admiration and happiness, Gilles is perhaps dreaming of the day when he will set off to explore the world for himself. (On the left, an eloquent symbol . . .

. . . of the party.) Brave Captain Thiercelin is warmly welcomed by the explorers.

A parallel picnic under the auspices of Belgian tourists.

At Saint-Rambert d'Albon children bathe and drink in the open air.

WHERE OUR DEAR READER WILL DISCOVER
THE FINAL RECKONING OF THIS SPIRITED EXPEDITION,
ALONG WITH OTHER EQUALLY IMPORTANT
AND ENJOYABLE DETAILS

As Vasco da Gama undoubtedly said somewhere, any expedition that takes itself seriously must give a clear account of its objective, for only in this way will it reach an undeniable scientific category, as is the case with the current one (end of sentence added by us).

However, that category will be raised to a level that can humbly be defined as sublime if the expedition has not one objective but two, in which case it will be met by the most overwhelming admiration, as undoubtedly will occur in the present circumstances.

The authors believe it their obligation to explain that, in the course of the preparation, they prudently considered only the first objective, in other words detailed knowledge of the freeway successively named the A6, A7 and Autoroute du Soleil, understanding it to be enough to create considerable commotion among their circles of friends and acquaintances, scientific as well as personal ones, divided from the beginning into two antagonistic camps, those who simply thought them mad and those who preferred to include them in the category of idiots. It's easy to imagine the reactions provoked by premature awareness of the expedition's second objective, which today, almost at the end of our obstinate safari, we can announce without emphasis but indeed with justifiable pride: it is to verify, at the end of the expedition, the existence of the city of Marseille.

Perhaps the first incitement to such an arduous enterprise came from the fact that all the travellers that leave Paris by the commonly known southern

For our part, after a bath, we turn Fafner into a clothesline, which the dragon tolerates amicably.

El Lobo startles la Osita while she is immersed in scientific speculations.

thruway do so with the assumption that at the end of their trip they'll be deposited by said thruway at the entrance to Marseille. This assumption, backed up by maps and other means of documentation, does not stand up to any serious analysis, for if Paris is certainly a known and provable element, since there the travellers start their cars and propel themselves towards the freeway access ramps, the opposite end is located more than eight hundred kilometres away, which rules out any empirical apprehension of the existence of the city of Marseille, which can only be retained as a theoretical piece of information provided by primary education, Fernandel, postcards from some aunt on vacation, the personality of Gaston Defferre and other elements that science can only take as working hypotheses and always, let's have the decency to admit it, with a pinch of salt.

Does Marseille exist?

That question must be answered in the final stage of the expedition when, having accumulated the multiple pieces of information about the freeway that our dear reader will find in this memoir, we'll be in a position to face up to our second objective and verify whether, after the last rest stop, we enter that city so casually accepted by travellers, or a vague region of barren ground and swamps, not to mention the possibilities of a shocking precipice or impenetrable forests.

What to think?

We won't prolong the doubt in the mind of our dear reader: Marseille exists, and it's just as Marcel Pagnol shows it. *But it only exists because the expedition has verified its existence*, and not for the reasons the masses accept, with no previous analysis.

We modestly think that this demonstration adds considerable weight to the results of our trip: the southern thruway is justified forever, and ceases to be the possibility of an enormous deception as we'd so often thought in our Parisian meditations, especially when we asked for authorization to explore it and did not receive an answer, something that struck us almost as proof of the non-existence of Marseille, and redoubled our determination to arrive at the truth no matter the cost, not to mention the expense of the tolls.

Breakfast: oranges, bread and butter, coffee.

9:14   Departure.

9:15   Col du Grand-Boeuf: 323 metres.

9:20   Stop: AIRE DU BORNARON.

Fafner facing: S. We set up on top of a little hill.

11:30   Visit from the gendarmes (they're nice, when they see us typing away they're overcome with deep respect, wish us luck and shake our hands).

Lunch: *escalopes de veau au citron*, salad (lettuce, peppers, onion), cheese, peaches, coffee.

17:20   Departure from this lovely rest area.

17:29   The Rhône valley on our right.

17:34   Stop: AIRE DU PONT DE L'ISÈRE.

It's not great, but it could be worse.

Fafner facing: E.

Dinner: ham and eggs, assorted cheeses, coffee.

THE TARTARS AGAIN,

AS IF WE DIDN'T HAVE ENOUGH TO DEAL WITH

"They've already had lunch, *che*," says a voice from behind the shrubs.

"Same old story," says another voice. "They must have radar to detect us, and even though it's still an hour before any decent person's lunchtime, these two dive into the mortadella and the wine just so there won't be any left for us. And after all we've sacrificed for them."

"*Mamma mía*, we've done nothing else for years now, and look how they thank us."

Recovered from the initial shock, la Osita invites them over, though they were already here anyway, and offers them each a glass of wine and what's left of the salami, which is quite a lot but disappears in a second. Up till now I've tried not to ask them questions that give them excuses to accuse me of all sorts of ingratitude and cold shoulders, but since it's been days since their last appearance, I feel obliged to ask them where they left their car.

"Car," says Calac, looking at Polanco as if he needed to visually lean on him so as not to tumble to the ground. "Hear what he asks me?"

"The freeway is generally reserved for cars," I point out in justification.

"For the cars of the rich," says Polanco, with the voice I imagine Karl Marx would use to say the same thing. "We poets live on moon beams and water, which is free in these places, fortunately."

"Salami is fuel as well," says Carol, who has far less patience with them than I do, which I understand perfectly, and which they return with silent, hostile glances.

"We," Calac informs me, "believe in our moral duty to follow you, in

At the Bornaron rest area, the exaggerated disorder testifies to the perceptible wear and tear on the explorers' energy reserves.

A vast and luminous solitude invites rest at l'Aire de Pont-de-l'Isère.

No one can know where we are, in the furthest reaches of the Pont-de-l'Isère rest area.

Childhood recovered: working on top of an enormous set of blocks . . .

spite of the suffering involved, to make sure you're not yet crazy enough to starve to death en route."

"Well said," Polanco approves. "Surprising vocabulary coming from you, but entirely appropriate in the context."

"I'm glad you've seen how well the expedition's going," I say to distract them from the mutual praise, which could go on for ages, "but you didn't answer my question. How the hell did you get here? I suppose you've been using other people's cars or something like that."

"We already told you it's torture," sighs Polanco. "Thumbing a ride, as the common people say, seems very easy given how nice and personable we are, cars stop as soon as they see us, but the problem is that every time we finish checking up on you, almost always in secret, we have to leave the freeway and come back the other way so we don't miss a single rest area."

"It's simply horrible," Calac chimes in. "You two advance by two rest stops a day, but the freeway exits are in the strangest places, so we have to hitchhike back, get out at a prudent distance, cross to the other side and wait for another car."

"I don't really understand," I say.

"Not to mention that as soon as they've picked us up, we have to ask to be dropped off in the very next rest area that appears, where you're sure not to be, but you never can tell, and then we have to wait for another car, and then another rest area, my God, my God."

"Don't let yourself get carried away," recommends Calac. "These two are going to end up thinking we actually take them seriously."

"You're right, brother," says Polanco. "I'm going to pieces from lack of protein and nights of insomnia, I could never sleep on the grass without getting hives."

Carol, who seems quite moved, goes to look for a couple of apples and suggests some hot coffee. I take advantage of her brief absence to amiably suggest that such selflessness is not absolutely necessary, especially since we didn't ask for it, and they'd be better off returning to Paris and sleeping in a bed for a couple of weeks. They, of course, give me that look I've known for so long. They love me, what can they do, it's not their fault they're so sentimental."

"See that," says Polanco. "They're kicking us out. If this torture . . ."

"I warned you," interrupts Calac. "Our dignity's at stake here, so as soon as we've drunk our coffee we'll be off."

"There is a bit of grappa," I say, feeling quite guilty.

"That doesn't change the situation," says Polanco, "although the protein issue obliges me to accept, a double if possible."

"And then we'll go on, since there aren't two little spaces in your vehicle."

"Even if it were just two tiny little corners," says Polanco.

"We're really very sorry," I say, knowing our fate is on the line at this very moment and if I let myself feel sorry for them we're going headfirst to hell, as almost always happens.

"You see," says Calac, putting as much sugar as possible in his coffee.

"Yes, it's our destiny," says Polanco who now has the bottle of grappa in hand. "It doesn't look like very good quality, look at the sediment in the bottom."

"They'll buy anything," says Calac. "I don't believe they'll make it alive to Marseille."

"We'll do what we can to protect you, but we can't promise anything. Maybe just one more glass, thanks."

"Careful, you're getting down to the sediment," Calac warns him. "I'll have the rest, though it may put my life in danger, but it's all I can do to protect you."

"You're a saint," says Polanco.

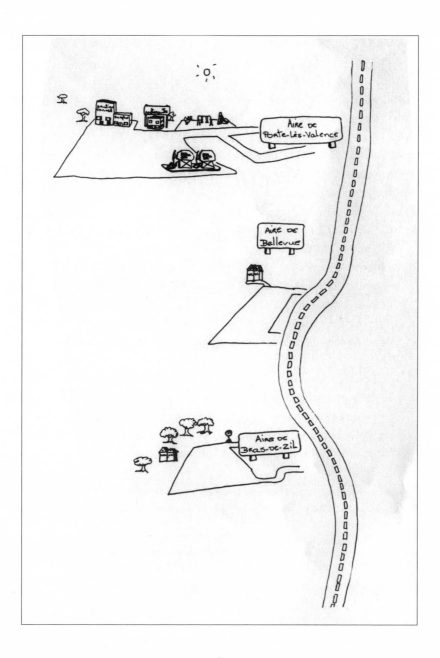

Breakfast: oranges, bread and butter, coffee.
9:00   18°C.
9:00   Departure under a grey and threatening sky.
9:05   Chateau de Crissol on our right.
9:12   Stop: AIRE DE PORTES-LES-VALENCE.
   Gasoline, restaurant, shop, children's playground.
   Fafner facing: S.
9:24   Departure.
9:30   Stop: AIRE DE BELLEVUE.
   Ugh! Nevertheless, we have a nice time.
   Fafner facing: S.
   Lunch: hard-boiled eggs, ham, salad (lettuce, tomatoes, peppers), cheese, peaches, coffee.
   Dinner: chicken soup, steak with lots of onions, peas
   and carrots, crème-dessert, coffee (in the restaurant).
At three in the morning we had to use the earplugs for the
second time in the trip. And it wasn't because of the roar
of the freeway, though it's right beside us, but due to
the constant and infernal racket of a refrigerated truck
that came to spend the night right behind us.

Where *la osita* speaks to *el lobo*
AND IT ALL GETS SAID FOREVER

The freeway is me, you, us, and when your tongue looks for mine and unwinds, escargot in escargot, your tongue slipping to infinity, unrolling at the back of my mouth, fragment of fragmented time, long ribbon of hot asphalt, then I too am escargot; your tongue stretches and I am a precipice, I swallow it and following that endless fever your face comes inside me, your hair, your eyes that blink in surprise, they think they're outside, they tickle as they open to an internal heat, you sliding in up to your elbows, swallowing you whole without stopping the kiss, first of many. Making room for you, the wet darkness half opens and you get as far as my belly, a thousand escargots dancing gravely in spirals, I am the other *coquille* as well.

We embrace forever until we can't breathe, looking beyond for a breath, you plunging without disappearing from where you are, your eyes on me and in front where the gaze has turned into a reflection of two, a thousand gazes, and you breathe me. I plunge like a pearl diver, tongue, no more than this tongue that lets itself be trapped, stretched, dragged along with this unquenchable thirst, the whole body that thins out to slide to the deepest, the most opaque, and spreads over your vehement softness. Still we search and still; how not to fall further than its, your, my tongue and the vertigo of the roads that lead there, always the same one and nevertheless there are slow routes, blazing roads.

A light that passes, a truck, the sounding of a horn; we absorb them in their turn with the suffocation, mouths sealed one against the other, upturning from outside on the other side. We invent the air where there is only moisture, heat and a night furrowed with lightning, and still I swallow your elbow, your other cheek, your sex that slips warm and living inside me and which I'll take for myself as well, you'll penetrate yourself because before declining to come back up to the surface, barely in time or perhaps too late, the suffocation has already started no doubt, the stillness of the voyage has already choked us in these essences of honey, of cinnamon, through Fafner winds stir nights, siestas, a thousand gestures to reach us; we are once again snails hiding in our shell that travels on the back of a wingless bird, will it be possible to arrive one day? When our bodies have already passed one into the other by tongue, when you are already a bird flapping at my breast, a snake encircling my hips from the invisible side of the skin, not a single cell escapes, confined from within to the moment when the blackness is striated with green stars, we have to go back, pant like we're almost out of breath but we're already out of breath, we can never recover our whole body before our mouths break away from each other with the violence of a strangulation. Breathe, but so little; you sink again, how to keep these inside-out bodies, turned like gloves sliding off hands that hold them back, and you sink, and like dolphins in a sea where we don't know the depths or currents, we slide one against the other, one in and around the other, and like sharks, wave after wave split to tear what remains of a reality that looks for something other than this rhythm.

From the beginning of the journey, of all journeys, measuring the immeasurable time from one crest to the next.

And in the damp abandon of exhaustion, peace, snail with a downy shell, your adolescent face that shines in its last efforts, and again with a tired hand but in the reflection of a next, still imperceptible, wave moves already, you draw me, my hips, breasts, bottom, and that drawing, gift from you to me, you give me once again the only gift of letting me leave you entirely and off to the lake of sleep that will rock us.

With a broken voice, more than once, you've said to me: "You're so young." You weren't wrong, but what veil keeps you from seeing all those years I too carry with me, years of an age much more than

"Don't speak to me of time!"

But yes, we talk, we who are not children; we are, we are in time as in this journey: inside. Don't you see there are no longer four or three or two times?

I've rushed into the black abyss so often that I know how to walk in the dark. And cutting off a thousand times, ten thousand times in a row the hydra's head, without kidding myself that I'll stop it from still and always continuing its sinister growing. Years believing or not in a birth made to let death get some sun, others spent dying it with vehement colours: we recognize each other.

For the moment, great sea wolf, we're rowing upon calm, clear water, stirred only by visions of shores where horrors, tortures and wars rustle and lie in wait. But our waves form only a vast undulation that breathes to the rhythm of our madness. Light and the dark passion will push us towards the end, always towards the end and further. There where I hold you as if our skin would dissolve at the contact of the other's, make of us a single invisible being.

Your voice is clear, but when that veil of sadness comes, when the journey has barely begun and you again doubt its end, how can I be silent, and how can I speak? In its time that sadness, my love, in its still distant and double time. As great as the darkness may be, there is no blackness that will make me retreat.

You, and still you.

By swimming in the great black waters, one learns to float in the dark. Buoy in the darkest night. Humiliating old age, health-care nightmares already ruled out; and the rest is not for now and there is no more possible solitude. Have you not understood what a gift of life it was that you didn't die a year ago? Cut. Departure. And the unknown that spreads out ahead for many years yet, if you want to explore it with your child-eyes.

Sweet confusion when the ground trembles in the sun and you vibrate against, in, around my body.

We won't leave the autoroute in Marseille, my love, or anywhere else. There's no turning back, only a spiral.

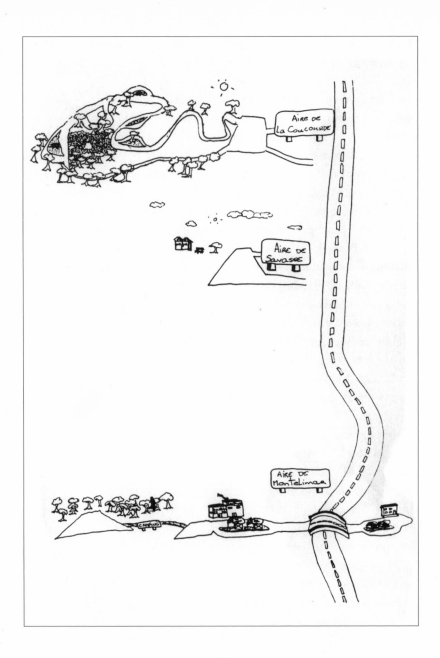

<u>Breakfast: oranges, almond cake and coffee.</u>

8:00 Looks like it's going to be a beautiful day.

8:10 Departure.

8:15 On our right, the mountains of the Ardèche.

8:16 Cross the Drôme River.

8:? Stop: AIRE DE BRAS-DE-ZIL.

Fafner facing: E.S.E.

<u>Lunch: chicken (sublime!), tomatoes, peppers, onions, pears in syrup, coffee.</u>

13:55 36°C.

14:00 Departure. Carol drives for the first time, and Julio takes over as navigator.

Zone de Montélimar.

14:10 Stop: AIRE DE LA COUCOURDE.

Lots of space and solitude, but trees are few and far between.

The parking lot is full of larks.

<u>Dinner: chicken with bamboo shoots, cheese, coffee.</u>

Rest Area of the Larks

Zwei Lerchen nur noch steigen
nachträumend in den Duft
Joseph von Eichendorff, *Im Abendrot*

Rest areas, monotonous? To us they seem more diverse all the time, we feel and experience them like microcosms where our red capsule touches down each day as if on undiscovered little planets. For example, La Coucourde, down by Montélimar, is a little country unto itself, and not only that but it's the country of skylarks, the first we've seen since leaving Paris.

Assuming they are skylarks, of course; birds aren't really our forte. La

At La Coucourde, the marvelous rest area of larks.

Tourists find nothing but space at La Coucourde, but the skylarks have made it their paradise.

The freeway teems with travellers, but at La Coucourde, emptiness and solitude reign for the happy explorers.

The "Teutonic Knights," always a little threatening for those who feel watched . . .

. . . by strange forces. A solitary "Teutonic Knight" guards the hills at Bras-de-Zil.

Osita reserves judgement but I am convinced, more out of courtesy than anything else. Poetry comes into play as well, and music especially, as will be seen, and childhood memories. Of course, in my suburban Argentine childhood there were no larks, but someone in the family said that skylarks sing mostly while in flight, the opposite of almost all other birds, and this peculiarity gave them a special prestige in my imagination; besides, they talked a lot about skylarks in *El Tesoro de la Juventud*, which was my inexhaustible stock of reality.

At the enormous and clear Coucourde rest area, where we're camping with the whole sky wide open over Fafner, since this afternoon that sky has been full of birds that climb and sing as they climb, they fly as high as possible and keep singing, confront the wind with a wonderful trembling of the wings and sing, and then descend singing and land in the trees and still sing, sing all the time and they are therefore skylarks, although deep down maybe not, but what can that matter to me while I listen with delight to skylarks singing in space?

The thing is, larks have always provoked arguments, and although I don't have my Oxford Shakespeare here (Fafner has his limits, poor thing), I remember, for example, the Verona lovers' night of romance, and the dialogue between Juliet and Romeo about whether the bird singing near the window is a nightingale or a lark. Here in La Coucourde there are no nightingales, that's certain, so the birds that fly and sing around us are larks; it seems a quite Shakespearean conclusion.

Lying face-up in my Florid Horror, I follow one lark on his ascent. He gains height in wide circles, small and brown and happy, he rises singing and his song is full, not too varied but constant and rich in colour, it seems to come from an incessant joy, as if the lark and his flight had no other raison d'être than this uninterrupted song, this celebration of life for its own sake, no reasons or ontology, no hells or heavens. Now almost a point in space, he stays motionless against the wind, his wings trembling in a crystalline suspension from which his song pours out and prodigiously arrives all the way down here. That tiny throat, that fragile little body, how can they be the source of a music exhaled hundreds of metres up in the air that comes to alight so clearly in my all but incredulous ears?

At that moment of contact, of perfect empathy, I'm overcome by the memory of Vaughan Williams' symphonic poem, *The Lark Ascending*. I cannot listen to it here, for the same reasons I can't read Shakespeare, and it's impossible to compare its melodic line to the one now descending from the sky, but its title confirms that the lark sings as he soars, that he ascends carried by his own music, as I believe no other bird does.

And then he comes sweetly back down, almost against his will, to rest on a branch, and Carol sees in him the shape of a phoenix, the body curved oddly downwards, seahorse of the air, wings beating ever more slowly until turning into an insignificant bird on a branch, a little creature that now looks like a sparrow or a thrush. Oh, how I wish I had Shelley here (*To a Skylark* is his, isn't it?), but it's been declared that I'll have none of my English friends at La Coucourde. It doesn't matter, they're skylarks, and this is the only rest area on the freeway with skylarks, a reserve chosen by them because the sky is high and wide, and maybe because one day we were going to arrive to celebrate them and larks are nothing but that, incessant celebration, like we are too in our own more obscure way, with words that would also like to be music, to be skylarks.

T*HE METAMORPHOSIS OF DREAMS*
ON THE FREEWAY

We did not intend to include the domains of Hypnos in these investigations; the double daily surveys of the rest areas seemed quite enough to manage. Maybe that's why at the beginning we didn't notice the changes; accustomed as we are to telling each other our dreams as soon as we wake up or whenever they decide to unexpectedly release their flashbacks, we kept on doing so here without noticing conspicuous changes. But four or five days after leaving Paris, we started to feel the first variations, which have become more and more accentuated.

The Florid Horrors know how to find the tiniest bit of shade under a merciless sky.

The explorers suspect the presence of a hidden microphone in the garbage can. They're still spying on us!

If we had to sum up the difference from our sedentary* dreams, we'd say it resides in a growing increase in acuity, of the way things and events stand out, the "lenticularity" of the images. We're dreaming ever less Rembrandt and ever more Van Eyck or Roger van der Weiden. When we tell each other our dreams, we start going into details with a strange precision, as much in reference to the scenery as to the storyline. We can't compare them, of course, but Carol's descriptions and mine these days have a meticulous texture, a very fine grain, intensely defined colours, complete and precise shapes. When we dream of people we know or knew, each feature, gesture

---

*Not that we're so still in Paris, just that our dreams always happen in the same habitat: room, bed, lights, atmosphere, sounds, etc.

La Osita also takes refuge in a little spot of shade while el Lobo cooks.

How chance placed one of his Florid Horror's daisies in el Lobo's hand.

and word have a startling fidelity, but if they're invented by the dream, that invention also has outlines and characteristics that could be called stereoscopic.

We wonder what can be causing this sometimes almost unbearable sharpening of our dreams. Among various hypotheses we have to take into account the novelty of the stimuli, which assumes a profound alteration in that sound box that is the unconscious with respect to what it receives through the senses while asleep. Dream quality probably also changes during an airplane trip or a night in a hotel, but since they are brief and isolated experiences, few take note. We, on the other hand, have spent three weeks inside a system of stimulation that is only modified partially (greater or lesser number of stimuli according to topography and nature of rest area), and in repeating itself night after night has ended up provoking a certain type of dream, which has finally prevailed upon our attention and our observations.

What I call the system of stimulation comprises, among other less verifiable things: the presence, lights and noises of trucks, as much in terms of the permanent traffic on the freeway as of their arrival, departure and parking in the rest areas where Fafner shelters our sleep. We spend very little time on the freeway, as our dear reader knows, but once in the parking lots we begin to see and listen to the trucks that come, as do we, to rest awhile or spend the night. We've already talked about the strange, fascinating ephemeral cities that form at night in some rest areas, where ten or twenty heavy cargo vehicles, not to mention cars with trailers or camper vans like Fafner, mingle license plates, languages, smells and sounds from multiple different countries. Enclosed in the capsule of Fafner, with his expandable canvas roof receiving the moving beams like a permanent magic lantern game, while the mechanical noises are like the more articulated foreground of the continuous clamour of the freeway, what stimuli never before concentrated around us unleash this different activity in the dream theatre? And why does this stimulation, unprecedented in our usual lives, outline so sharply the silhouettes of our dreams, why does it focus rather than blur them?

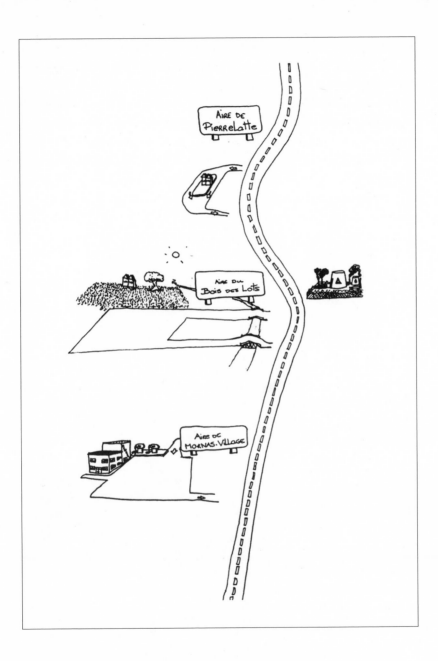

Unanswerable questions, but meanwhile we dream in a different way and we like it, we like it more and more even if we dream the horrors that befit any normal being. No need to add that as soon as we return to Paris we'll be attentive to what happens in the well-known atmosphere of our home; if dreams let us down, as we fear, we'll have to think up new and varied expeditions. The world, after all, is full of rest areas where perhaps await dreams of such richness that they'll be worth all the outbound journeys and, one of these days, even a journey of no return.

<u>Breakfast: oranges, green tomato preserves, coffee.</u>

(?) It's already afternoon. For the second time we've lost track of time.

(?) Departure.

Germans have fully taken over the role of the English, and their numbers are even greater. A real invasion!

(?) Almost immediately: Stop: AIRE DE SAVASSE, very small and no shade.

Fafner facing: S.W.

A few tables and a WC.

(?) Departure.

<u>Lunch: chicken salad with orange slices, tomatoes with onions, peaches.</u>

(?) On the right, the foothills of the Southern Alps.

(?) Ten kilometres further on, stop: AIRE DE MONTÉLIMAR.

Gasoline, restaurant, tourist office, nougat for sale. Showers! (Illegible phrase).

Also: wooded picnic spot, with paths for the cars.

15:00 Sitting on the terrace of the café, trying to recover from the oppressive heat, we see André Stil and his wife Odette, who sit down at the next table. A bit of pleasant chat.

<u>Dinner: steak-frites, strawberry tart, coffee (in the restaurant).</u>

Last night, after the final sadnesses of the stupid Malvinas War, *France-Inter* gave us the gift of a program no true explorer could ever afford to miss. A team as scientific as ours (*honni soit qui mal y pense!*) were transmitting from Scotland, from the banks of Loch Ness, a detailed report about Nessie, the charming aquatic creature that has been submerging and reappearing in our imaginations for a century and a half, though in the loch itself she does so much less often.

That was how a learned man described as a "crypto-zoologist" tried to convince us that the plesiosaur hypothesis is quite weak, but that he is con-

At Montélimar rest area we run out of our provision of books, and have to resort to magazines from the shops.

vinced of the existence of a group of giant seals or sea lions, since a single Nessie is biologically impossible. Someone called Tim Teasdale alluded to his balloon explorations over the lake, to the film when Nessie proved herself a star of the seventh art, and even a "yellow submarine", which I don't think is the same one that brings back pleasant memories of the Beatles (who could forget the charming Jeremy or the sinister Glove who looked so much like a South American general?).

From that erudition it turned out that there's more and more proof that Nessie lives in Loch Ness, and that in Lake Champlain, between Canada and the United States, she has a distant cousin, not to mention another who frolics with glee in Loch Morlach. I silently chip in another link to this chain of friendly and inoffensive monsters; I remember in my youth there was much talk in Argentina of a plesiosaur that had stuck its head above the waters of one of our austral lakes more than four times. While twenty million Argentines laughed at the supposed monster (they who believe in so many two-legged plesiosaurs), I fondly remembered Dr. Onelli, who not only defended his conviction till his death, but was also the director of the zoological gardens in Palermo Park. Now English and French experts support him indirectly by indicating that all the lakes where the existence of such enormous creatures has been noted are found in regions where the average temperature is around ten degrees, as is the case with the lakes of Patagonia. Dr. Onelli did not have sonar, radar and other similar implements at his disposal, but last night's program ended almost certain that Nessie would soon be identified, along with all her family who, it has to be said but with no offence intended, have been pulling our legs for long enough.

Carol and I went to sleep hoping to be able to join one of the next expeditions for reasons more magical than scientific, and the aura still hovered around us this morning in the next rest area where we'd set up the Florid Horrors in the scant shade of a rather mutant little tree. At a certain moment I discovered the moon in the middle of the bright blue eleven-in-the-morning sky; I was looking tenderly at its shy waxing quarter, which always moves me if I see it in broad daylight because the moon always looks smaller and extremely defenceless, when off to the right I clearly distinguished a transparent sphere almost motionless in space. Carol came like a shot when I shouted, and confirmed the sight; I ran to get the binoculars (observe the advantages of an expedition as scientific as ours), and with them we could see the sphere perfectly and it looked like glass, it had no gondola, and didn't give the impression of being anything other than that, a transparent sphere, which was already quite something.

Since we've read a lot about UFOs and other space Nessies, I rushed over to an innocent Swiss family that was eating at one of the tables and practically replaced the rotund gruyere sandwich the stunned head of the group was eating with the binoculars. Instead of punching me, he condescended to look up and then pass the binoculars to his wife and children. They all said the same thing:

"You're right, it's a transparent sphere."

I confess I'd hoped for something more, but in any case now I had the necessary witnesses in case the vision took on other characteristics or hinted at a landing. But no; the sphere slipped gently into the distance, and a cloud covered it forever. A weather balloon? Possibly, but I've seen several and they weren't perfect glass spheres. Glass? Yes, glass. Carol and I saw reflections that no plastic, no matter how polished by the boys in the observatory, is capable of producing. So as Nessie is in her lake, that sphere is in some part of the sky; since last night we've become part of some no-man's-land of reality, and now things like this happen as naturally as any other event of the trip. After all, the Swiss family was right not to be startled.

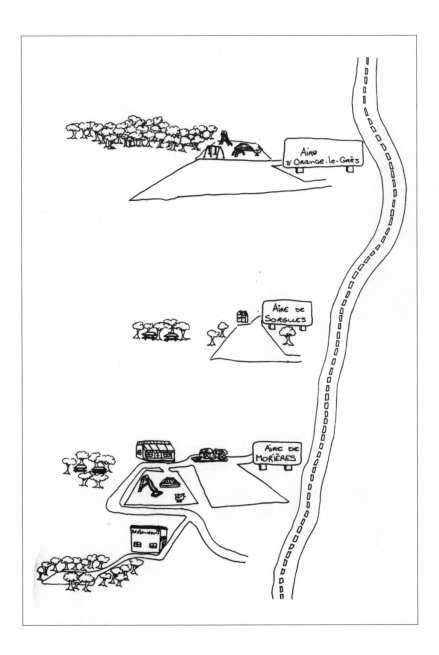

In the middle of the expedition we get this news. Amazement, enthusiasm, drink a toast.

Later we wonder if this M. Rickart is the same person we asked for authorization for our indefatigable venture, and who replied with a cadaverous silence. We'd written to the Director of the Public Highways Authority, while M. Rickart is the President of the Association of French Highways

Authorities. Oh, mystery. Maybe it's not the same one but it doesn't matter. In mid-expedition, fate, which is the method preferred by cronopios, approves ex post facto a cultural initiative that we have de facto embarked upon, damn it, since those cursed bureaucrats took no notice of us. And now they want artists! M. Rickart cries out for the freeway to be beautified. Who or what could beautify it better than our delightful chronicle? Artists of the pen, painters of atmospheres, sculptors of privileged moments erected forever upon pedestals of words, so every user of the autoroute can carry in their glove compartment the aesthetic condensation of that black ribbon they travel, of those green islands (most of the time) where they'll stop for relaxation and their favourite sandwiches. Have we not anticipated your desires, M. Rickart? Are we not giving modern-day France a good example of how the imagination can truly take power if we forget about routines?

We anxiously await your authorized opinion, since we never heard anything from the other guys.

At l'Aire de Pierrelatte they also monitor us in strange disguises . . .

Breakfast: apricot juice, croissants, butter, jam, coffee.

10:00   Overcast. 20°C.

15:12   Departure from the picnic area.

15:25   Departure from the shop, where we buy a few necessities.

15:35   Stop: AIRE DE PIERRELATTE.

Fafner facing: S.

Lunch: chicken with mayonnaise, crème "Grand Marnier", coffee.

Small rest area with two tracks (trucks and cars), with no shelter or shade.

15:40   Departure.

Large and wonderful sign: YOU ARE IN PROVENCE.

15:45   Stop: AIRE DU BOIS DES LOTS.

Fafner facing: S.

Unexpected and comforting arrival of Brian Featherstone and Martine Cazin. Great drinks and chat.

Dinner: macaroni à *la forestière* with ham, crème "Grand Marnier", coffee.

Expeditionary Cultural Soirées

One of the most often repeated ways of ending the day is that after dinner la Osita settles into Fafner's back seat, using it as a bed, and after lighting the gas lantern starts stubbornly reading things like the diary of Virginia Woolf, while I go up to the driver's seat and turn on the transistor, plug in my headphones, and armed with numerous cassettes give myself a concert that is always sort of a résumé of myself, that is to say rather whimsical, absurd, contradictory, illogical; in other words, music the way I've always understood and loved it, to the scandal of my serious musicological friends.

A visit as unexpected as it is pleasant at the Bois des Lots rest area: Martine Cazin and Brian Featherstone descend from their hills to encourage us on the last leg.

Almost at the end of the expedition, I wonder about the reasons that dictated my selection of cassettes. It's very good, but I don't always understand why. I did it in a rush, and that perhaps explains why there are three works by Lutoslavski and none by Boulez, three cassettes of Billie Holiday and none of Ella Fitzgerald or Helen Humes. It doesn't matter, there's more than enough for the trip. Tangos, for example: Carlos Gardel with a selection that includes *Malevaje* and *Mi Triste Noche* (in the good version, mind you), Ángel Vargas, Pugliese, Julio de Caro, and a selection of the more villainous classics that Tato Cedón gave me that includes Rosita Quiroga, Corsini, Magaldi, Charlo . . . I also have a whole cassette with the voice of Eladia Blázquez singing her songs that these days, at the end of this imbecilic and sinister war in the South Atlantic, seem even truer: *Somos como somos*, *Patente de piola*, *Vamos en montón* . . . But also there, and also so true for me, are *El corazón al sur* and *Por qué amo a Buenos Aires*.

I'll never know how I brought three cassettes of Fats Waller and only one of Ellington and one of Armstrong; I'm not making value judgments, but it's funny to find an hour of music by Charles Mingus and another of Jelly Roll Morton against barely ten minutes of Lester Young; I think I was half asleep that morning, although thank heavens I remembered to bring the best of Bix and Trum, which sounds so clear, so trimly perfect in the rest area nights. And there's also Schubert's quartets numbers 804 and 887, played by the Juilliards, and Arnold Schönberg's first quartet. But in the end I think I was right to overdo it on the Lutoslawski, because it's what I listen to most and best these days. There is something in his prodigious String Quartet, in his Music for Thirteen Instruments, which chimes marvelously well with the sonorous atmosphere of the rest areas where the sound of the freeway is a mere backdrop for birds, insects, broken branches, all that also feeds into the texture of the music, although the musicologists won't believe it.

Oh, and I also have Susana Rinaldi singing Cátulo Castillo and Homero Manzi like no one else can.

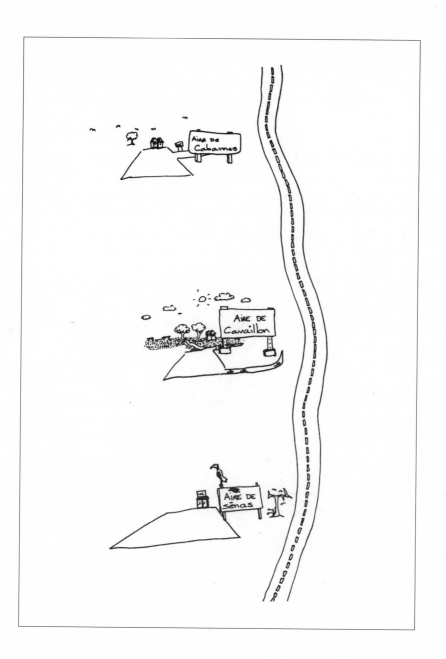

After parking her yellow 2cv in front of Fafner, she brusquely opens the door and goes around to the other side of the car, where she proceeds to eat standing up, at once energetically and as if in hiding, bending towards the car to fill a spoon with who knows what, shooting nervous glances in our direction as if we were going to jump on her or announce over a loud-speaker that EATING IS A SIN (meanwhile, back at the ranch, we stuff our-selves without the slightest shame or hurry; then will come coffee, siesta, and the lady in the yellow 2cv will be replaced by a little Ford, then a big truck, until eventually we lose count).

Suddenly (how quickly she's eaten, we say to one another, but we're wrong) the lady slams the door and, armed with a small rectangular bag and a larger one that she hangs on her shoulder, strides purposefully towards the shop behind which we've parked. Stunned, I see her return a few seconds later: without slowing her pace, holding onto her bags as if fearing an attack at any moment, she's already been around the building. Once. Twice. Is she a hired killer in search of her prey (why *two* bags?)? An illiterate who can't find the WC? Or is she expecting an arm to reach out suddenly from the door above which is written "Truckers' Lounge", grab her and drag her towards swarthy, exciting strangers? (What goes on in a "truckers' lounge" anyway? And in all those cabs with the curtains pulled down?)

However, no one springs from the shadows to suddenly change her life. Did she fall in love with a truck driver when she was twenty? Has she travelled the freeways ever since in the hope of someday finding her beloved? Would she recognize him after all this time? Her raven-haired hero may well have gone grey, or baldness may have transformed him entirely. Authors of certain romance magazines would certainly find ample

Lost in the jungle? L'Aire de Bois-del-Lots seems to be waiting for Tarzan . . .

. . . and also for Jane, naturally, for whom it reserves flowers and birds.

inspiration if they explored the freeways like we do. And if the reason for having taken off like a shot is more ordinary and necessary, she'll have to hold it till the next rest stop since she doesn't appear to have found the WCs either. She returns to her car with the same quick step, almost without lifting her feet off the ground, opens the right-hand door and continues her almost military mastication as if nothing had happened.

And then, adjusting her dress that's too long and too wide beneath her jersey, which appears to have decided at the very last minute not to be a shawl, smoothing her grey hair, she gets back behind the wheel and leaves.

In slippers.

Fafner beneath the trees. A washing line strung up and very full. In the distance, a village whose bell tower seems to sway in the evening mist. On this side, a table with typewriters, books, papers, pens, cups of coffee. Evening encroaches, bides its time.

Without knowing why, the light reminds me of the beginning of a story sketched out during a conference in Poitiers, and which must still be in my bag. Surprise upon rereading it, having just spent most of the afternoon reflecting on photography, way of seeing, manner of seeing, to force the

You might need a magnifying glass, but between the two posts is a beautiful hoopoe who provided us with friendly company and bade us good luck.

tearing of one reality too often superficial and perhaps even deceptive, if the gaze is no more than a negligent and fleeting glance: It was about the angel of Poitiers, authentic creature of the light. I'm still not sure those who were in the restaurant with me really saw it. Only a photograph, perhaps, and I didn't have my camera with me, could have let it be seen as I saw it. How does this transformation work, that passage from the subjective power of the eye to what is photographed? It's not simply a question of technique but rather, to begin with, of knowing how to see, and then how to impregnate the objective "reality" with the same gaze. Just as literature cannot be explained as the simple management of words – since at least in societies called developed the whole adult population makes use of "techniques" of written language – the attraction and magic of photography cannot be explained by technical know-how. When you get right down to it, do the photographer and writer not participate in a single process, just using different tools?

But the transformation of the story of the angel – making it pass from the untaken photograph to the written fiction – will take some time yet.

Orange-Le-Grès: how to imagine what this was going to reveal?

But we have to bow before the evidence, as will be told in good time.

Breakfast: oranges, madeleines, walnut spread, coffee.

Sunny and windy day.

8:22 Departure.

8:23 Enter Dèpartement de Vaucluse.

8:28 On the left, Le Rocher de Mornas.

8:29 On the left, the Mornas Fortress (11th century).

8:37 Stop: AIRE DE MORNAS-VILLAGE.

Fafner facing: E.

Gasoline, shop, restaurant, and an enormous quantity of tourists.

8:50 Departure.

9:00 Stop: AIRE D'ORANGE-LE-GRÈS.

Excellent wooded rest area. We find solitude among the trees. Yes, but . . .

Fafner facing: E.

A whole day and night of total peace.

Lunch: sardines, mackerel fillets, tomatoes, peppers, onions.

Dinner: spaghetti with butter (Carol) and olive oil (Julio), crème-dessert, coffee.

WE MUSTN'T BELIEVE IN WITCHES
BUT THEY EXIST, THEY EXIST

Orange-le-Grès . . . Who would have suspected? Such a rich name, mixing the juice of the fruit with the earth that the hands of the earliest men turned into glasses, statues, sacred figures . . .

Ah-ha. Statues, sacred figures? Explorer, explorer, nothing like letting yourself get carried away by poetry, I mean by associations between words and things: from an orange and clay comes what we're trying to say in another way, certainly less well. Because in this rest area, which is beautiful and spacious and has nooks where we and Fafner find a slow, fresh solitude, in this rest area lives the Devil. As always, under the appearance of a garden of delights, though it may be much more modest than Bosch's. And, as always, only to innocents will it be given to discover the truth and recount it later so that everyone mocks and doesn't believe them. (We don't care. We don't care. We'll say it anyhow.)

The trick is simple, like all good ones (see Houdini and other experts). For years and years travellers have found signs saying WORKS IN PROGRESS on many stretches of road, followed by a zone where red and white plastic cones (there are different models, but they all clearly resemble a witch's hat) which indicate the narrowing or blocking of a route. Yesterday, when we arrived at the Orange-le-Grès rest area, we saw the cones piled up beside the entrance, as if later on they were going to close it or finish reopening it. We didn't pay much attention, and after sheltering Fafner under the trees and discovering that the rest area was enormous, we began to walk

Impossible to deny we've come face to face with horror...

around to carry out the scientific annotations the reader already knows and admires.

Like other rest stops, this one has an area arrived at by following a series of signs that say CHILDREN'S PLAYGROUND. The games seemed to be varied, rustic, nice. Seemed to be. They seemed varied, rustic and nice until the illumination. Games for children – those constructions with thick planks for bases, those shapes that inevitably evoked another kind of game based on horror and suffering? Everything came together in a second, and we knew the truth: we were in the place where witches are punished and executed, and the rest area was a masterpiece of camouflage designed to hide what only an expedition and long experience like ours could discover.

I hope the photos give an idea of the gallows, scaffolds and instruments of torture that were in the square. It is here where the witches are executed in various ways, and later they are taken to different freeways and buried

. . . which is confirmed to us by the gallows.

Even the most innocent mushrooms worry us now, so close to the gallows.

upright, as an ancient sanction dictates, leaving their hats over the graves, as a chastening lesson to other witches. Now we understand: the hats piled up at the entrance of the rest area are undoubtedly an agreed upon sign for the next meeting of judges, executioners and members of the public selected to witness the *autos-da-fé*, in which for obvious reasons they have substituted the scaffolds and gallows for the bonfires (it's well known that it's illegal to light fires in the rest areas). Without doubt, when the appointed day arrives, the hats will be arranged in a line to close the entrance to Belgian, English and domestic tourists who travel this section of the autoroute, something that will come as no surprise as our dear reader can attest in the light of what happened to us at the beginning of the expedition. A rest area closed to the public has no apparent importance; much more important is the discovery that it's closed so inquisitors can use it to execute a new contingent

A case of diabolical possession? After the terrible discovery at Orange-Le-Grès, el Lobo seems overcome by strange forces.

of witches, whose number appears to increase constantly in France, judging by the quantity of hats disseminated over all the principal highways and byways of the country.

So then, do we have to suppose that the *Malleus Maleficarum* forms part of the practical bibliography of the freeway, along with the Michelin Guide? Is the government of François Mitterand, especially the cabinet, going to stand by with their arms folded at this revelation? Is this socialism? What is Christiane Rochefort waiting for? When will the literary fire-bomber write a book about this? And the *Editions des Femmes*? Practically all witches are women and inquisitors men. *Usque tandem, Catilina?*

The WC at Orange-Le-Grès
tries to disguise the dark
reality of the rest area with
its hospitable little figures.

Breakfast: oranges, madeleines, green tomato pre-
serves, coffee.

We decide to stay in this enchanting place until after
lunch.

Lunch: rice with butter, crème-dessert, coffee.

14:30 Departure (with tears in our eyes).

14:32 Mont Ventoux on the left.

14:35 Cross the river Ouvèze.

14:40 Stop: AIRE DE FOURNALET.

Fafner facing: S.S.E.

Small rest area, with a bit of shade and tables, but only
accessible to pedestrians.

16:00 52°C. Departure.

16:12 Stop: AIRE DE MORIÈRES.

Gasoline, restaurant, picnic tables, playground.

We discover a second parking area, lovely and secret,
right by the exit from the main parking lot. Avignon can
be seen in the distance.

Dinner: mixed salad, *entrecôt*, mashed potatoes (her),
rice (him), compote, coffee.

Expeditionary discipline: a month into the strenuous voyage, Fafner's interior is still orderly and clean.

SLEEPING OSITA

I presume a good explorer tends to wake up at dawn to make various scientific observations corresponding to the day as it begins. It must be for that reason that I too almost always wake up very early, but instead of getting up and consulting the various instruments Fafner is equipped with, I stay agreeably in the house and devote myself to the study of a subject that Vespucci, Cook and Captain Cousteau never even attempted, in other words: la Osita's manner of sleeping.

This manner of sleeping is perhaps that of all little bears, something which would be impossible for me to verify, for which reason I shall take care not to make imprudent generalizations. In Osita's case, her sleep goes through two principal stages, the first of which is not at all extraordinary: Osita finds the most comfortable, most agreeable position, covers up depending on the atmospheric temperature, and for most of the night sleeps very naturally, almost never face up and almost always face down, with lateral intervals that never last long but which give way to other positions with no effort whatsoever, after gentle movements that reveal the depth and pleasure of her sleep.

When dawn arrives, in other words the time when I tend to wake up entirely, for the preceding observations have actually been made without too much scientific rigor, I notice quite soon that Osita has entered the second stage of her slumber. It is here where one might well ask whether this manner of sleeping is all her own or if it extends to the entire species, since it seems quite unusual, even extraordinary behaviour, consisting of continuous attempts the sleeping Osita makes to turn herself into a parcel, a bundle or a package, which contains everything, thanks to a series of movements, gestures, tugs, pulls and tangles, that progressively wrap her up in the sheets until she turns into a big white, pink, or blue and yellow striped cocoon, depending on the situation, to the point where a quarter of an hour after the beginning of this daybreak metamorphosis, which I always contemplate in amazement, Osita disappears in a twisting confusion of sheets, which gradually disappear from my side of the bed, by the way, for no one could imagine the strength Osita employs in drawing them to her, until she manages to get entirely involved in them and finally keeps still after one last series of evolutions that complete the chrysalis and the evident happiness of its occupant.

Leaning on my elbow on the mattress, which is all that's left, I tenderly watch Osita and wonder what deep need to return to the womb or something similar her determined labour every dawn responds to. I know very well (because at the beginning I didn't know and was frightened) that none of this rejects me, for all I have to do is brush the warm parcel at my side with a finger to get a soft growl of satisfaction to emerge from its depths.

Scientific workstation inside Fafner.

The mystery is complete, as you can see, because Osita is content to feel me at her side and at the same time take refuge in a cloister I cannot enter without destroying its precious darkness, its intimate temperature, and something within her knows it and defends it from daybreak till she wakes. Once – not anymore – I tried to unwrap her as gently as possible from the cocoon, because I was afraid she'd suffocate in the tangled sheets and confused pillows, and I found out what it meant to separate her hands from the knots, bonds and other not so loose ends of the sheets between her fingers. So now I only watch her sleep in her ephemeral and undoubtedly atavistic hibernation, and wait until she wakes of her own accord, when she begins to extricate herself little by little, to get a hand out, a trickle of hair, a bit of her rump, or a foot, and then she looks at me as if nothing had happened, as if the sheets were not a huge whirl around her, the broken chrysalis from which peeks out my new day, my reason to live a new day.

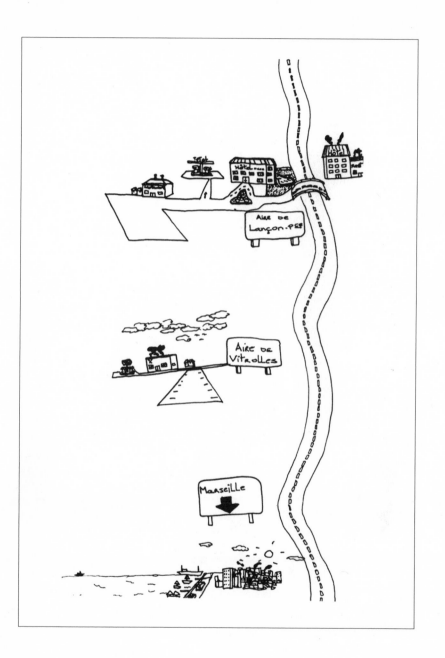

EXTRACTS FROM THE POCKET GUIDE TO LOBOS

They are polyglots and like music.

◇ ◇ ◇ ◇

A white wolf less than thirty centimetres high or more than three and a half metres tall has never been seen.

◇ ◇ ◇ ◇

Offering garlic to a white wolf is not recommended, it could make him mistake himself for a wolf of a completely different family.

◇ ◇ ◇ ◇

Not normally fussy when it comes to diet, the white wolf has a particular and limitless loathing for cucumbers.

◇ ◇ ◇ ◇

If you tickle him, he laughs wholeheartedly. As for other caresses, see the Pocket Guide to Ositas, "Lobos" chapter.*

◇ ◇ ◇ ◇

*This manual should be written down but the reader will forgive el Lobo for guarding it only in his memory.

This genus of wolf is capable of the worst insanities, which are usually the most beautiful.

◇ ◇ ◇ ◇

If you intend to show off at a cocktail party by pronouncing sentences like: "Why don't we catch the Orient Express tonight", make sure you pack a suitcase first, because they don't sell toothpaste or panties on that train.

◇ ◇ ◇ ◇

You should only tell him horror stories by day, unless you want to have nightmares yourself.

◇ ◇ ◇ ◇

He has very long arms, which provide certain advantages in some circumstances, and very agreeable ones in others.

◇ ◇ ◇ ◇

Whatsoever his date of birth, he has the imagination, vivacity and perversity of childhood well-anchored in the depths of his gaze. To live with a Lobo, it is necessary to understand that all watches are renewable artichokes.

◇ ◇ ◇ ◇

In general he shows certain genius for cookery, although he may sin by excess of imagination. If you know he intends to bake an apple pie, for example, it is prudent to hide the jars of paprika, basil, coriander and thyme.

◇ ◇ ◇ ◇

Warning to those who fear intoxication: do not breathe too deeply at his side.

◇ ◇ ◇ ◇

Contrary to popular opinion, el Lobo has skin silkier than newborns, with the additional advantage of not smelling of milk.

◇ ◇ ◇ ◇

Unlike most animals of the species, the white wolf presents a breach in his immunological defences, through which the world passes. Accept the burden of part of this weight, otherwise the breach could turn into a malignant sore. (If the same type of fissure exists in his soul, don't be frightened, it won't multiply his worries, but quite the contrary.)

◇ ◇ ◇ ◇

He is frequently seen in the company of a dragon.

◇ ◇ ◇ ◇

When el Lobo wakes up in a good mood, whether at five in the morning or three in the afternoon, he unfailingly tends to share his enthusiasm with those (or rather with her) around him: Fair warning to grumpy sleepy-heads who take their time emerging from the morning mists.

◇ ◇ ◇ ◇

El Lobo has a confirmed tendency to dance in the woods, especially when there are stars.

◇ ◇ ◇ ◇

Protect his feet while he sleeps; maybe he'll give you a dream as a gift, or he'll sing some Schubert from the depths of his slumber.

◇ ◇ ◇ ◇

When necessary, gently scorn his machismo, and little by little he'll lose it.

◇ ◇ ◇ ◇

Breakfast: grapefruit juice, brioches, croissants, butter, jam, coffee (in the buffet).

13:30 Departure.

13:35 We cross the Durance.

Enter Département de Bouches-du-Rhône.

13:37 Stop: AIRE DE CABANNES.

Fafner facing: E.

Hideous rest stop, especially after the last one.

13:38 Departure.

13:40 On our left, the Luberon mountains.

13:44 Stop: AIRE DE CAVAILLON.

Fafner facing: E.

Lunch: *grive entière fourrée* (gift from Brian and Martine), chickpea and onion salad, exotic fruit salad, coffee.

20:30 Arrival (announced on the previous visit) of Raquel and Jean Thiercelin, Doña Pura, Raquel's mother, Vladimir (friend of Jean's who bet we'd never complete the journey), and Gilles Thiercelin.

Great reunion and dinner at a picnic table.

Dinner: boiled eggs, *rôti de porc*, cheese, strawberries, lots of wine, coffee.

At the Cavaillon rest area, now near our goal, we receive an extra visit from Captain Thiercelin and his crew (in the foreground, Vladimir, who is mentioned in the text).

And the party goes on till nightfall, thanks to the delicious provisions supplied by Raquel, seen here next to Doña Pura, her mother.

Remembrance of a Friend,
of how fafner came into our life
thanks to this friend, and other things
that also have to do with poetry

It was fair and necessary that among my reading for the trip I should bring the Journals of Paul Blackburn, my friend the poet who died more than ten years ago. *The Journals*, edited by another American poet, Robert Kelly, contain the poems that Paul was writing in the last two or three years of his much too short life. But in fact all his poems, all his previous books, are also journals, because what gives Paul's poetic voice its depth is the deliberate lack of distinction between supposedly poetic and prosaic subjects; like other New York poets, to Paul poetry was knowledge and at the same time interpretation and immediate transfiguration of daily experience, cats and seagulls, women and window blinds, airplanes and wasp stings, countless car journeys, highways, farms, Provençal troubadours – who he loved and translated admirably – hotel and motel rooms, loves and distances, cities and pigeons.

I say this reading (rereading, for the most part, since Paul had sent me many of the poems in *The Journals*) is fair and necessary to our work, because the origins of this expedition can be traced as far back as the day Paul revealed to me the wonders of a dragon, Fafner's twin brother, and I realized that riding a dragon one could discover the lands and beaches and forests of Europe in a new way. What from outside had appeared to be a Volkswagen like so many others, opened its cave and revealed its liberating riches the very day Paul arrived at my shack in Saignon in the Vaucluse valleys full of lavender and almonds.

I can't say that Paul's house on wheels was a model of order, to begin with because he was travelling with his wife and his sister, and three people are too many for a dragon designed for two and at most a baby skilfully neutralized in a hammock prepared for such a purpose; also Paul was travelling with an enormous Mexican sombrero from which he did not want to be parted under any circumstance and which alone took up a third of the space inside the dragon. As if this weren't enough, books, papers, dictionaries and notebooks filled all the spaces functionally reserved for other ends by the House of Volkswagen, whose technicians would have recoiled in horror had they been able to see the use Paul and the girls made of the various constituent parts of the camper van.

And nevertheless, all I had to do was peek into the dragon, see how the back seat turned into a bed, how the little hand pump spilled water into a sink while the little gas stove sputtered away enthusiastically to cook eggs or spaghetti, for the illumination to arrive, and with it the future changed, all without me being aware of it in that Provençal present where Paul had brought his laughter, his marijuana and his cassettes, along with the complete works of The Beatles, and where for several weeks we worked together to tighten up his translations of some of my short stories into English, and sang and talked and travelled around all the adjacent valleys, and experienced all that Paul tells in his poems about Saignon and what I tell in a few chapters of *Around the Day in Eighty Worlds*, where there are also (bad) photos showing Paul and his wife Joan, showing Julio Silva, showing the living and the dead and the absent, showing all the rivers that sooner or later will end up in the sea, Jorge Manrique. But I'm writing this as Paul would have liked it, as he always wrote, fully within life at every moment, and neither of us are going to go getting melancholy, because that would seem like a betrayal.

Just that I would have liked to send him these lines and say: You see, when you left you didn't know you'd illuminated me, that I'd go back to Paris and at one of the worst moments of my life thanks to you I'd do the exact opposite of what any right-thinking person would do, in other words instead of sinking into the neurosis that already enlightened so many of my friends, I went to find myself a dragon, taking advantage of a totally unexpected cheque that arrived from some foolish editor, I went to find a red dragon, I named him Fafner as a real and red dragon must be named, and as soon as I figured out how to drive him, bought some cans of food and bottles of wine and boxes of Kleenex and filled the water tank to wash my face in the mornings, and I went to Austria, crossing all of France and Germany and learning to sleep in Fafner, to cook in Fafner, sure, keeping things a little tidier than you did, without any enormous sombreros or two hundred pocketbooks thrown all over the place, but just like you with a transistor radio and lots of cassettes, just like you with a book by Gary Snyder, I remember, and so, in a way, the conditions piled up so that one day, so many years later, when la Osita also came to know and love Fafner and almost immediately discovered things I'd never even suspected about him (for example, a mosquito screen for the back door, which had travelled inside Fafner for ten years without me noticing it), when the two of us decided that a forest was worthless if it wasn't a forest with Fafner in its most secret corner, and that beaches are a heap of sand and water if Fafner isn't there to organize them, give them their meaning and their true lines of escape, at that time the idea of the expedition was born after a long battle with the demons, but I think Osita has already told about that somewhere else, so I'll just remember how you, Paul Blackburn, already so close to that departure that still strikes me as impossible, a mere delay in the correspondence that we'll soon catch up on, how you taught me that trips need to be poems and for that one needs a dragon, this one beside us among the trees who's watching me write with his big corrugated glass eyes, having a well-earned rest in this wood full of birds and fuzzy caterpillars.

Breakfast: oranges, biscuits, coffee.

8:40   45°C.

8:41   Departure.

8:44   We stop right on the freeway due to a technical fault: we'd forgotten to fold down the roof.

8:50   Stop: AIRE DE SÉNAS.

Fafner facing: E.

Sinister rest area.

9:00   Departure.

9:01   On the right, the Alpilles mountains.

9:05   Toll. We pretend for the second time to have lost our ticket and we get through without problems, after paying 85 francs.

9:20   Another toll: 5 francs.

9:21   Stop: AIRE DE LANCON.

Fafner facing: S.S.W.

Hotel, restaurant, gas station, tourist office.

We check in to the hotel.

Lunch: Parma ham, faux-filets frites, salad, cheese, coffee (in the restaurant).

Dinner: Carol forgot to record it. We ate in the hotel.

WHERE THE EXPLORERS HAVE THE PLEASURE
OF PRESENTING FACSIMILE REPRODUCTIONS
OF THE TWO TOLL TICKETS, WHICH FOR
REASONS ALREADY KNOWN TO OUR READER THEY
HAD "LOST" WHEN THE TIME CAME TO PAY

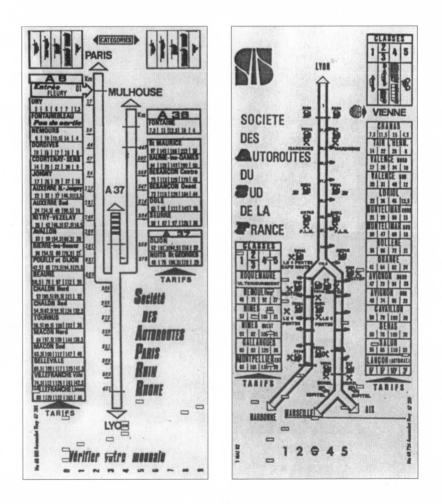

340

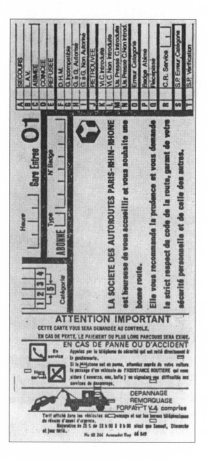

A	SECOURS
B	L.A.V.
C	ABIMEE
D	CONGEE
E	REFUSEE
F	D.H.M.
G	G. Incompatible
H	G. à G. Autorisé
I	G. à G. Non Autorisé
J	RETROUVEE
K	V.C. Introduite
L	V.C. Non Introduite
M	Us. Presse C.Introduite
N	Us. Presse C.Non Introd.
O	Erreur Catégorie
P	Badge Abimé
Q	Récépissé
R	C.R. Service
S	S.P. Erreur Catégorie
T	S.P. Vérification

Heure   Gare Entrée **01**

Type   N° Badge

ABONNE

Catégorie   1 2 3 4 5

LA SOCIETE DES AUTOROUTES PARIS-RHIN-RHONE

est heureuse de vous accueillir et vous souhaite une bonne route.

Elle vous recommande la prudence et vous demande le strict respect du code de la route, garant de votre sécurité personnelle et de celle des autres.

ATTENTION IMPORTANT

CETTE CARTE VOUS SERA DEMANDÉE AU CONTROLE.

EN CAS DE PERTE, LE PAIEMENT DU PLUS LONG PARCOURS SERA EXIGE.

EN CAS DE PANNE OU D'ACCIDENT

En service — Appelez par le téléphone de sécurité qui est relié directement à la gendarmerie.

Hors service — Si le téléphone est en panne, attendez auprès de votre voiture le passage d'un véhicule de l'ASSISTANCE ROUTIERE qui vous aidera (essence, eau, huile) ou signalera une difficulté aux services de dépannage.

DEPANNAGE REMORQUAGE FORFAIT T.V.A. comprise

Tarif affiché dans les véhicules dépannage et sur les bornes téléphoniques de réseau d'appel d'urgence.
Majoration de 25 % de 18 h 00 à 8 h 00 ainsi que Samedi, Dimanche et Jour férié.

Ho 68 244 Aussedat Rey 66 849

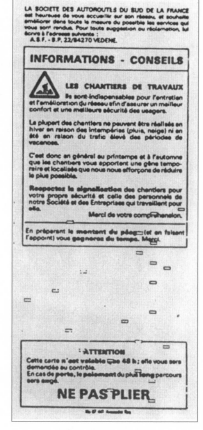

LA SOCIETE DES AUTOROUTES DU SUD DE LA FRANCE est heureuse de vous accueillir sur son réseau, et souhaite améliorer dans toute la mesure du possible les services qui vous sont rendus. Pour toute suggestion ou réclamation, lui écrire à l'adresse suivante :
A.S.F. - B.P. 22/84270 VEDENE.

INFORMATIONS - CONSEILS

LES CHANTIERS DE TRAVAUX

Ils sont indispensables pour l'entretien et l'amélioration du réseau afin d'assurer un meilleur confort et une meilleure sécurité des usagers.

La plupart des chantiers ne peuvent être réalisés en hiver en raison des intempéries (pluie, neige) ni en été en raison du trafic élevé des périodes de vacances.

C'est donc en général au printemps et à l'automne que les chantiers vous apportent une gêne temporaire et localisée que nous nous efforçons de réduire le plus possible.

Respectez la signalisation des chantiers pour votre propre sécurité et celle des personnels de notre Société et des Entreprises qui travaillent pour elle.

Merci de votre compréhension.

En préparant le montant du péage (et en faisant l'appoint) vous gagnerez du temps. Merci.

ATTENTION

Cette carte n'est valable que 48 h ; elle vous sera demandée au contrôle.
En cas de perte, le paiement du plus long parcours sera exigé.

NE PAS PLIER

Ho 67 441 Aussedat Rey

At l'Aire de Sénas, we're surprised to find roofed enclosures for tourists' meals.

Explorers the Way We Like Them

I'm going to visit the penguins
and offer them a concert by phonograph.
We've done it already several times
successfully, but this time the effect
will exceed anything imaginable.
I'll make then listen to "Ouvre tes yeux
bleus, ma mignonne" *that my*
excellent friend Lasalle had
sung especially for
us before our departure,
and it seems the penguins can
appreciate the talent of this great artist,
since one of them tried to get
inside the speaker, probably
to hear better. I also wanted
to record the voice and cries
of the penguins, but the result
was virtually useless.

Jean Charcot, *Around the South Pole*

DRAGONS NEVER LIVE IN PEACE,
BUT THEY CAN BE HELPED

Poor dear Fafner gives us the impression of feeling a bit humiliated when the Italian camper van pulls in beside him. Suddenly he looks very small, dirty and absurd with his roof raised; he looks like the dragons painted by most of the artists of the Renaissance, who presented them looking defenceless before the bulk of Saint George's horse and the dimensions of his lance. What can Fafner do against an opulent Fiat, which, as if it weren't enough in itself, rubs it in by wearing license plates from the very country whose artists, from Paolo Uccello to Rafael, have already humiliated so many dragons?

To avenge him, to stand by him more than ever, I begin to study the five tinpot Saint Georges who take their baskets and bottles and settle down at a table, fortunately distant from us, who with our habitual cunning have quickly taken possession of the best spot in the woods. Three men and two women dive into a far from frugal picnic while I reflect that the Fiat is obviously quite large and could shelter two couples like so many apartments or studios in Paris or Milan; but five people seems a bit much, and I wonder how they spend the nights, three and two, four and one, or all five together, with all that can suggest to a not overly timid imagination. Once again the rest areas open up to any hypothesis, fertile ground for erotic suppositions, duty-free zone for mobile *Decamerons*, taking from place to place their varied amorous constellations, their fixed-term pacts (maybe in Lyon or in Avignon there will only be two or three passengers left in the Fiat, or another will join one of these days, the one missing for the perfect hexagon . . .).

Fafner, of course, doesn't think about any of this, but I feel my critical focus on his Italian competitor helps him to feel better. He may be small but he's with us, a little dragon but a happy one with us two who occupy just the right spot in his heart, exactly the diastole and systole he needs to have no fear or envy of his Italian fellows.

<u>With the excitement (and sadness) of the final stage,</u>
<u>Carol forgot to note the gastronomic details of the</u>
<u>last day.</u>

9:55 Departure.

10:10 A sign full of significance for us: YOU ARE NOW
LEAVING *L'AUTOROUTE DU SUD DE LA FRANCE*. BON VOYAGE.

10:11 On the right, l'Étang de Berre.

10:12 On the left, the Vitrolles cliffs. On the right,
Marignane Airport.

10:14 Stop: AIRE DE VITROLLES.

Fafner facing: W.

Gas station, shop.

On the periphery, a gypsy camp.

10:16 Departure.

We enter the zone of air pollution.

10:30 WELCOME TO MARSEILLE.

10:35 Nôtre-Dame-de-la-Garde comes into view.

10:38 FREEWAY ENDS.

10:40 Arrival at the old port, where we stop at the Marcel
Pagnol Quay.

Final documentary photos. Our triumph does not make us as
happy as we'd expected, quite the contrary. We're hurt by
the din of the city, the smells of the port, the reinte-
gration in temporal affairs that already demands we
hurry, rush up to Serre (but there we'll rest for a few
more days of peace), and return to Paris, seeing our
islands fly past in so few hours, the marvelous archipelago of the rest areas now separated from us by the oncoming lanes, out of reach, oblivious, far away . . .

HOW QUICKLY THE TRIP WENT BY!

We knew it, of course: the end of great expeditions or heroic exploits or feats of prowess is commonly seen as the apotheosis, from the crowning with laurel of the ancients to the Olympic medal of our days and even the cheque that awaits the winner in four sets or fifty circuits of the track. But the end of our trip was – logically more than commonly – the opposite of an apotheosis, to such an extent that I'm only writing these final lines many months later, and I write them without any desire to write them but obliged not to abandon our patient and pale reader who has travelled with us all these pages.

Sadness: that's what there was. A sadness that began two days before the arrival, when at the Sénas rest area we looked each other in the eye and for the first time fully accepted that the next day we would enter the final stage. How can I forget Osita saying: "Oh, Julio, how quickly the trip went by . . ." How can I forget that at the moment we read the sign announcing the end of the autoroute we were so filled with anguish we could only combat with an obstinate silence, which accompanied us till we entered the clamour of Marseille, looked for an empty spot in the Vieux Port and put our feet on land that was now no longer Paris–to–Marseille land. A triumph clouded by tears we dried in a café, drinking the first Marseille *pastis* and thinking that this very afternoon we would drive up to Serre for a few days' rest at the Thiercellins' house, our generous port, always our land of refuge.

Last stage: we leave the autoroute and advance towards Marseille. A month without seeing oncoming traffic!

Marseille: At the Vieux-Port, seagulls line up to receive the expedition with full honours.

"Mommy, when does the last car come onto the freeway?"

(Stéphane, at three years of age.)

Now I wonder: was it not in some way ours, Osita?

Exhausted but victorious, we complete our voyage on a dock whose name provides the most fitting reception possible.

WHERE, TO FINISH, THEY HINT AT

OTHER POSSIBLE REASONS FOR OUR

EXPEDITION AND PERHAPS ALL EXPEDITIONS

When the secret was no longer secret, when back in Paris our friends gathered round to be amused by the oral version of the trip, waiting for the book that would complete what we told them between laughs and jokes, a different version of the trip emerged in many comments. Almost immediately there were those who wanted to know if our intentions had been simply playful or if behind them lurked a different sort of search, the immersion in a landscape not merely geographical, the confrontation with ordinary life and with that defiant no-man's-land established in the middle of the frantic pace of civilization. Someone wanted to know if we hadn't put into practice a contemporary form of Zen provocation, if the sometimes exasperating going against the grain of a trip opposed to all the possibilities proposed and favoured by the freeway had as its true aim an interior encounter, a liberation of tensions of a personal and even historical order, if Marseille were not our Grail, our Orplid, our land of Urkhalya as perhaps our dear José Lezama Lima might have put it.

All that dazzled us a bit, but most of all we found it funny, because we'd never conceived nor realized the expedition with underlying intentions. It was a game for a little Bear and a Wolf, and that's what it was for thirty-three wondrous days. Faced with disturbing questions, we said many times that if we'd had those possibilities in mind, the expedition would have been something else, perhaps better or worse but never that advance in happiness and love from which we emerged so fulfilled that nothing, afterwards, even admirable travels and hours of perfect harmony, could surpass that month outside of time, that interior month where we knew for the first and last time what absolute happiness was.

And maybe for that very reason we understood wordlessly that perhaps we *had* carried out the trip obeying unbeknownst to us an interior search that would later take on different names in the mouths of our friends. We understood that in our own way we'd performed an act of Zen, we'd looked for the Grail, we'd devised the golden domes of the Orplid. And all that had happened precisely because we hadn't thought of it nor looked for it nor proposed it, because love and joy filled us too much to leave any room for a searching anxiety. We had found ourselves and that was our Grail on earth.

POSTSCRIPT, DECEMBER 1982

Reader, maybe you already know: Julio, el Lobo, is finishing up and putting this book in order alone, this book which was lived and written by la Osita and him the way a pianist plays a sonata, the hands united in a single quest for rhythm and melody.

As soon as the expedition was over, we returned to our activist life and left once more for Nicaragua where there was and is so much to do. Carol resumed her photography work there while I wrote articles to show on all possible horizons the truth and nobility of the struggle of those people who tirelessly continue their journey towards dignity and freedom. There too we found happiness, no longer alone in the rest areas of Paris–Marseille, but in daily contact with women, men and children who looked forward as did we. There Osita began to decline, victim of a malady we thought passing because the will to live in her was stronger than all the prognoses, and I shared her bravery as I'd always shared her light, her smile, her love of sun and sea, and her hope for a more beautiful future. We returned to Paris full of plans: finish the book together, donate the royalties to the Nicaraguan people, live, live even more intensely. There followed two months that our friends filled with affection, two months in which we surrounded la Osita with tenderness and in which she gave us each day that courage that we were gradually losing. I watched her embark on her solitary journey, where I could no longer accompany her, and then on the 2nd of November she slipped through my fingers like a trickle of water, without accepting that the demons would have the last word, she who had so defied and fought them in these pages.

I owe it to her, just as I owe her the best of my final years, to finish this story alone. I know very well, Osita, that you would have done the same if it had fallen to me to precede you in the departure, and your hand writes, along with mine, these final words in which the pain is not, never will be stronger than the life you taught me to live as perhaps we've managed to demonstrate in this adventure that comes to an end here but goes on and on in our dragon, goes on forever on our freeway.